Federico García Lorca
Plays: One

Blood Wedding,
Doña Rosita the Spinster, Yerma

Spain's most celebrated dramatist, an outstanding theatre director and a significant poet and artist, Federico García Lorcia was murdered by Nationalist partisans in 1936 at the outbreak of the Spanish Civil War.

The three tragedies included here were all written at the height of his powers and display his innovative mix of Spanish popular tradition and modern dramatic technique. Set in his home territory, Granada, the plays return again and again to the lives of passionate individuals, particularly women, trapped by the social conventions of narrow peasant communities.

Blood Wedding (1933) signalled Lorca's growing fame at home and abroad. Based on the true story of an Andalusian couple escaping a prearranged marriage, it is Lorca's most famous and poetic play. *Yerma* (1934) is a more austere piece illustrating the savage claustrophobia of a small village. This translation by Peter Luke was first staged at the National Theatre, London. *Doña Rosita the Spinster* (1935) centres on one of Lorca's favourite images, the stages of a rose in bloom, a metaphor for life's passing.

Federico García Lorca was born in 1898, near Granada, the son of a wealthy farmer. He studied in the Faculties of Arts and Law at the provincial university before moving to the Residence for Students, a prestigious college in Madrid, during a period of intellectual and artistic ferment. He travelled in the USA and South America in 1929 and 1930, and in 1931 was made director of the touring theatre company La Barraca by the Republican government in Spain. He was murdered by Nationalist partisans in 1936. Because of his habit of reading his work aloud to friends, many plays and collections of poetry were published long after they were written. He published several books of poetry: *Book of Poems* (1921), *Songs* (1927), *Gypsy Ballads* (1928), *Poem of Deep Song* (1931) and *First Songs* (1936). His stage plays include: *The Butterfly's Evil Spell* (1920), *Mariana Pineda* (1927), *The Shoemaker's Wonderful Wife* (1930), *Blood Wedding* (1933), *The Love of Don Perlimplín* (1933), *Yerma* (1934), *When Five Years Pass* (rehearsed reading, 1936) and *The House of Bernarda Alba* (private reading, 1936).

by the same author

Lorca Plays: Two

The Shoemaker's Wonderful Wife
The Love of Don Perlimplín
The Puppet Play of Don Cristóbal
The Butterfly's Evil Spell
When Five Years Pass

Lorca Plays: Three

Mariana Pineda
The Public
Play Without a Title

FEDERICO GARCÍA LORCA

Plays: One

Blood Wedding
Doña Rosita the Spinster
translated by Gwynne Edwards

Yerma
translated by Peter Luke

Introduced by Gwynne Edwards

Methuen Drama

METHUEN DRAMA WORLD CLASSICS

9 10 8

These translations first published in Great Britain in 1987 by
Methuen London Ltd

Reissued with a new cover design 1993, 2000
Reprinted 2006

Methuen Drama
A & C Black Publishers Limited
36 Soho Square
London W1D 3QY
www.methuendrama.com

ISBN 978-0-413-15780-5

Printed and bound in Great Britain
by Good News Digital Books, Ongar

Contents

Federico García Lorca: A Chronology

1898   Born on 5 June in Fuentevaqueros, near Granada, the eldest of the four children of Don Federico García Rodríguez, a prosperous farmer, and Doña Vicenta Lorca Romero. An illness at two months prevents him from attending school until he is four. Educated at home by his mother.

1902/3   The family moves to Valderrubio, near Fuentevaqueros. Lorca goes to school.

1909   The family moves to Granada. Lorca attends the College of the Sacred Heart.

1914   Begins his studies at the University of Granada in the Faculties of Arts and Law, without enthusiasm.

1915   Studies piano and guitar, attends the Conservatory and gives some private recitals. Friendship with Fernando de los Ríos, Professor of Political Law at the University. Begins to attend literary gatherings at the Café Alameda in Granada.

1917   In spring and summer educational visits, organized by Martín Domínguez Berrueta, Professor of Art Theory at the University, to different cities and regions of Andalusia and Castile. A meeting in Granada with Manuel de Falla further stimulates Lorca's love of music.

1918   Lorca publishes his first book, *Impressions and Landscapes,* based on the trips of the previous year.

1919   Lorca leaves Granada for Madrid and commences a ten-year stay at the Residence for Students. Amongst his close friends are Luis Buñuel and Salvador Dalí, champions of the *avant-garde.* Lorca strives to conceal his homosexuality. Writes his first play, *The Butterfly's Evil Spell.*

1920   *The Butterfly's Evil Spell* staged at the Teatro Eslava in Madrid, 22 March. Closes after four performances.

1921   Publication of Lorca's first volume of poetry, *Book of Poems.*

1922   Gives a lecture on 'deep song' at the Granada Conservatory. With Manuel de Falla, Lorca organizes the Festival of Deep Song, which is held in Granada on 13 and 14 June.

1923   Presents with Manuel de Falla a children's play festival
        celebrated at the Lorca household in Granada and
        including his own puppet play, *The Girl Who Waters the
        Basil Plant.*

1924   Friendship with the poet, Rafael Alberti. Works on poems
        to be published subsequently in *Songs* and *Gypsy Ballads,*
        and on his play, *Mariana Pineda.*

1925   Visits the home of Salvador Dalí at Cadaqués, north-east
        Spain. Friendship with Dalí's sister, Ana María. Reads
        Mariana Pineda at the Dalí home.

1926   Lectures in Granada: 'The Poetic Image in Don Luis de
        Góngora'. Writes the first version of *The Shoemaker's
        Wonderful Wife.*

1927   Edits the first number of the literary magazine, *Cockerel.*
        Publishes *Songs,* his second volume of poetry. Première of
        Mariana Pineda, to considerable acclaim, on 24 June at
        the Teatro Goya in Barcelona. Exhibits drawings at the
        Galerías Dalmau in Barcelona. *Mariana Pineda* opens in
        Madrid on 12 October at the Teatro Fontalba.

1928   Publication of *Gypsy Ballads,* to become Lorca's
        best-known volume of poetry. Lectures in Granada:
        'Imagination, Inspiration and Evasion in Poetry'; and
        'Sketch of Modern Painting', with illustrations of pictures
        by Dalí and Miró. Lectures at the Residence for Students:
        'Lullabies'. Completes *The Love of Don Perlimplín.* He is
        increasingly depressed. Involvement in an affair with a
        sculptor, Emilio Aladrén.

1929   End of the affair with Aladrén. June marks the beginning
        of a nine-month visit to the United States. Enrols as a
        student of English language at Columbia University.
        Spends August at Eden Mills in Vermont and September
        at Newburgh, before returning to New York.

1930   Works on *The Shoemaker's Wonderful Wife* and the
        poems that would form the volume *Poet in New York,*
        published in 1940. Arrives in Cuba in the spring, works
        on *The Public* and *When Five Years Pass.* Returns to
        Spain in the autumn. Première of *The Shoemaker's
        Wonderful Wife* at the Teatro Español in Madrid on
        24 December.

1931   Publication of *Poem of Deep Song.* Completes *The Public*
        and *When Five Years Pass* and works on the puppet play,

The Puppet Play of Don Cristóbal. Under the auspices of the new Republican government becomes director of the touring theatre company, *La Barraca*.

1932   Tours with *La Barraca*. Reads *Poet in New York* in Barcelona.

1933   Première of *Blood Wedding*, directed by Lorca, at the Teatro Beatriz in Madrid, 8 March. A huge success. Première, 5 April, at the Teatro Español, of *The Love of Don Perlimplín*. Collaborates in May with Manuel de Falla on a production at the Residence for Students of *Love the Magician*. Works on *Yerma* and directs *La Barraca*. Travels to Argentina in September and directs *Mariana Pineda*, *Blood Wedding* and *The Shoemaker's Wonderful Wife* in Buenos Aires. A triumphant enterprise.

1934   Returns to Buenos Aires in March to direct his adaptation of Lope de Vega's *The Foolish Lady*. Continues to direct *La Barraca* in Spain. Writes *Lament for Ignacio Sánchez Mejías*. Première of *Yerma*, to great public and critical acclaim, 29 December, at the Teatro Español.

1935   Production of an extended version of *The Shoemaker's Wonderful Wife*, 18 March, at the Teatro Coliseum in Madrid. Performance, directed by Lorca, of *The Puppet Play of Don Cristóbal*. Production of *Yerma*, 17 September, in Barcelona, and in the same city, on 13 December, triumphant première of *Doña Rosita the Spinster* at the Teatro Principal Palace. Has also commenced work on *Play Without A Title*.

1936   Publication of volume of poetry, *First Songs*. Declines invitation to Mexico to direct his plays. Completes *The House of Bernarda Alba* on 19 June and reads it to his friends on 24 June. The Theatre Club Anfistora rehearses *When Five Years Pass*. Second private reading of *The House of Bernarda Alba* on 15 July. On 16 July Lorca leaves Madrid for Granada. Military insurrection, led by Franco, on 18 July. Granada falls to the military, 20 July. Lorca hides in the house of the poet, Luis Rosales, is arrested on 16 August, detained in the Civil Government building. In the early hours of 19 August he is driven away and shot in the head outside the village of Viznar by members of the Assault Guard and the paramilitary 'Black Squad'. His body was never found.

Introduction

Federico García Lorca was born on 5 June 1898 in the village of Fuentevaqueros, near Granada, the eldest of the four children of Don Federico García Rodríguez and Doña Vicenta Lorca Romero. His father, a prosperous farmer, was a strong and active man who in later years would accept only reluctantly his eldest son's dedication to poetry and theatre. Doña Vicenta, on the other hand, was a former schoolteacher whose interest in Federico's early education proved to be crucial, for the fever which struck the boy down at two months affected his early attendance at school. Crucial too in relation to his development as a writer was his childhood contact with the Andalusian countryside, its people and its customs, all of which were an endless source of fascination to him. From his mother and the household servants he became familiar with the songs and stories of southern Spain that colour so strongly his poems and plays. His theatrical interest was stimulated too by the gift of a toy theatre. Surrounded by family, servants and local children, he presented entertainments of his own devising, manipulated the puppet figures, designed the costumes and controlled the whole performance in a way that already anticipated his future role as dramatist-director.

The family move to Granada itself in 1909, when Federico was eleven, was important in many ways. This fascinating city, distinguished by its exotic mixture of Arabic, Greco-Roman and gypsy tradition and boasting amongst its architectural delights the Palace of the Alhambra, became in a sense Lorca's real birthplace and would occupy a central position in all his mature work. In addition, Granada was a city of culture, especially of music, and it allowed Lorca, under the guidance of Don Antonio Segura, to develop and display to a wider public his considerable talent as a pianist. An important consequence of this was an initial contact with the increasingly famous composer, Manuel de Falla, which led eventually to lasting friendship, a mutual interest in traditional Spanish music, and collaboration in the presentation of some of Lorca's puppet plays. Furthermore, Granada contained many other highly talented people who would influence the young man in different ways: Fernando de los Ríos, Professor of Political Law at the University, was one of the most distinguished humanists and scholars of the day; Martín Domínguez Berrueta, Professor of Art Theory, encouraged the writing of Lorca's first book, *Impressions and Landscapes*, published in 1918; Juan Cristóbal was a talented sculptor; Angel Barrios and Andrés Segovia were brilliant guitarists; José Fernández Montesinos was a well-known literary critic, and José Mora Guarnido a successful journalist. At the same time Granada received amongst its foreign visitors writers and musicians as famous as H.G. Wells, Rudyard Kipling, Wanda Landowska and Arthur Rubenstein. It was little wonder that the teenage Lorca should be inspired by such talent, and he was clearly further stimulated by the regular literary meetings that took place at the Café Alameda where many of Granada's 'bohemian' set discussed their current plans and projects. On the other hand, this was a time in which Lorca's awareness of his homosexual tendencies fostered in him a sense of frustration and isolation – very evident in *Book of Poems* (1921) – and when others too became conscious of that aspect of his character to which a predominantly 'macho' society would react with hostility and horror. Significantly, his brother Francisco omitted all reference to Federico's homosexuality in his important book, *Federico and his World*, published as recently as 1980.

In April 1919 Lorca left Granada for Madrid where he entered the Residence for Students, an academic institution of great prestige modelled on the Oxbridge college system and founded nine years previously. When Lorca arrived, Luis Buñuel had already been at the Residence for two years and they soon became close friends, and 1922 saw the arrival of Salvador Dalí. The names are sufficient to conjure up an impression of the excitement, intellectual stimulus and creative energy with which the Residence abounded in those days, and there were others, too, connected in one way or another with the building: the poets Emilio Prados and Rafael Alberti; the musicians Ernesto Hallfter and Gustavo Durán; the writers José Bergamín and Rafael Martínez Nadal, and frequent foreign visitors such as François Mauriac and Igor Stravinsky. Needless to say, the various 'isms' of that time, from Dadaism to Surrealism, were debated with enthusiasm, the writings of Freud were seized upon by eager minds, and the creative writers and artists of the Residence, often neglecting their formal studies, threw themselves with abandon into their own projects. Lorca was to remain there for ten years and produce much of his best work, especially poetry.

The question of Lorca's homosexuality evidently pre-occupied many of his friends, even in an atmosphere as liberal and open as that of the Residence. Given the nature of Spanish society and its hostility towards homosexuals, Lorca did little to draw attention to himself in that respect, and some of his closest friends appear not to have been aware that he was in any way different. Others, however, suspected him and, in the words of José Moreno Villa, 'kept their distance'. One of the residents, Martín Domínguez, appears to have spread rumours about Lorca which on one occasion prompted a disturbed and dis-believing Buñuel to confront him directly with the question: 'Is it true you're a queer?' Buñuel has described Lorca's sense of hurt and shock, but he did not answer the question and Buñuel himself insists that there was nothing effeminate about him. Pepín Bello, another close friend, has emphatically denied that Lorca was homosexual, though he notes that he did not share most of the other students' obsession with the opposite sex. The evidence suggests the extent to which he managed to conceal his homosexuality, for there is little doubt that he did have homosexual relationships. His close friendship with Salvador Dalí contained a strong element of sexual attraction on his part, if we are to believe Dalí's subsequent affirmations, but there is no suggestion of an actual physical relationship between them. For the most part Lorca's feelings were clearly suppressed, but his sense of frustration and uncanny understanding of the female mind were both to surface in his plays.

The performance of Lorca's first play, *The Butterfly's Evil Spell*, took place in Madrid on 22 March 1920. The hostile reception of a work whose characters are a butterfly, cockroaches, a scorpion and glow-worms was a bitter blow to him, and when he returned to stage-writing with *Mariana Pineda*, completed in 1925 and premièred in 1927, it was not with a subject that was risky or a treatment that was boldly *avant-garde*, but with the traditional story of a liberal heroine of Granada, her opposition to the King, Ferdinand VII, her doomed love for another liberal, Pedro, and her final execution. The play's success compensated for the earlier failure. In 1926 Lorca started work on another play, *The Shoemaker's Wonderful Wife*, first performed in 1930 and then in a revised form in 1933, while in 1928 he completed *The Love of Don Perlimplín*, premièred in 1933. In both plays Lorca employed a traditional subject – the young wife married to a much older man – expressed in the traditional forms of puppet play and farce, but there is clear evidence now both of a new confidence in his own ability and of a desire to push beyond the limitations of tradition. On the one hand, farce often slips into tragedy. On the other, Lorca's stage technique, combining setting, costume, movement, dialogue, music and lighting, is part of that exciting theatrical experimentation of the first quarter of the century, exemplified by such European innovators as Maeterlinck, Yeats and Edward Gordon Craig.

As far as Lorca's other writing is concerned, the 1920s saw the publication of three volumes of poetry: *Book of Poems* in 1921; *Songs* in 1927, and the outstandingly successful *Gypsy Ballads* in 1928. His fame grew too with the important lectures he gave in these years, especially, 'The Poetic Image in Don Luis de Góngora' and 'Imagination, Inspiration and Evasion in Poetry', but towards the end of the decade he became strangely and deeply depressed. Whatever the cause – and a homosexual relationship with a young sculptor, Emilio Aladrén, has been suggested – the decision was taken that Lorca should leave Spain for a while. In the summer of 1929 he arrived in New York with his friend and former teacher at the University of Granada, Fernando de los Ríos.

New York, far from lifting Lorca's spirits, presented him with a spectacle of tasteless commercialism and, in the case of the Blacks of Harlem, of people oppressed by their poor circumstances, removed from their natural environment, and often attempting to imitate their white masters in a desperate effort to improve their lot. Unable to speak English – his few phrases included 'Tim-es Esquare' and 'ham and eggs' in a thick Spanish accent – Lorca found himself largely alienated and isolated in a city markedly different from his beloved Granada, and was glad to escape to Cuba in the spring of 1930. Nevertheless, the New York experience led to the composition of three very striking and ambitious works: the difficult but moving poem, *Poet in New York*, first published in its entirety in 1940; and the two extremely bold 'surrealist' plays, *The Public* and *When Five Years Pass*, completed in 1930 and 1931 respectively, and which Lorca regarded as being far ahead of their time.

His return to Spain in the summer of 1930 coincided with the fall of the seven-year dictatorship of Primo de Rivera, while the election of a republican government in 1931 created an atmosphere of political and artistic freedom in which Lorca's talents flourished as never before. His appointment in 1931 as director of a government-sponsored touring theatre company, commonly known as *La Barraca*, allowed him to perform to rural audiences many of the great plays of the 'classic' Spanish dramatists Lope de Vega, Tirso de Molina and Calderón and, more importantly, to evolve a style of performance involving music, dance and simply stylized sets that shook off the dust of years of stuffiness in relation to their presentation. The inter-relationship of Lorca's experiments with *La Barraca* and his own creative writing cannot be over-emphasized, for nowhere is the mix of Spanish popular tradition and modern dramatic technique better exemplified than in the four great plays written at this time: *Blood Wedding* (1933), *Yerma* (1934), *Doña Rosita the Spinster* (1935) and *The House of Bernarda Alba* (1936). With the performance of *Blood Wedding*, Lorca became the most celebrated Spanish dramatist of his day, acclaimed in his own country and in South America. At the same time he continued to write poetry, notably the great poem of 1934 occasioned by the death of a bullfighter friend, *Lament for Ignacio Sánchez Mejías*, and the poems, influenced by Arabic poetry, that would become the *Diván del Tamarit*.

By the beginning of 1936 the hopes that had accompanied the inauguration of the Second Spanish Republic five years earlier lay in tatters and the country found itself in a state of political crisis. When, on 18 July, Franco's military rebellion against the Madrid government set the Civil War in motion, Lorca was in Granada. It was not long before the rebel troops occupied the city and, with the eager assistance of fascist supporters, began to 'clean up' the town and its surrounding areas. Lorca's brother-in-law, Manuel Montesinos, mayor of Granada and a steadfast supporter of the Republic, was one of the first to be shot, and Lorca himself was soon obliged to take refuge in the house of a friend and fellow-poet, Luis Rosales. On the afternoon of 16 August he was arrested and taken to government headquarters where he was held for two more days. From there he was driven away, probably in the early hours of 19 August, and shot in the countryside outside the village of Viznar. In a time when political and personal differences were inextricably mixed, the combination of Lorca's republican sympathies, his homosexuality and his enormous fame was more than sufficient to afford his enemies the opportunity of ridding Granada and Spain of one of her most illustrious sons.

II

Blood Wedding, undoubtedly the greatest of Lorca's plays, was read by the dramatist to his friends on 17 September 1932, and premièred at the Teatro Beatriz in Madrid on 8 March 1933. Acclaimed by theatre critics and public alike, it signalled his growing fame at home and abroad, was soon translated into French and English and was performed in both the United States and South America. It is, clearly, the play on which Lorca's international reputation has been built and yet, for more than twenty years after the end of the Civil War, political circumstances, the general stagnation of the Spanish theatre, the nature of Lorca's death and the opposition of his family prevented the performance of any of his work in Spain. *Blood Wedding* was not presented there again until 10 October 1962, and there have been few productions since. It is a curious fact in this respect that Lorca's play has achieved more publicity in recent years through Carlos Saura's film of Antonio Gades's flamenco-dance version which, good as it is in its own right, omits Lorca's marvellous last act. In 1986 *Blood Wedding* was, however, performed both in Spain and at the Edinburgh Festival by the company of José Luis Gómez in a production which clearly did justice to the play, and was much praised by Michael Billington in the *Guardian*: 'Grieving motherhood and Greek sense of fate are also at the centre of Lorca's masterpiece *Blood Wedding*; and José Luis Gómez's spare, lean, highly musical and deeply moving Madrid-based production at the Royal Lyceum captures a sense of tragic inevitability.' As far as productions in English are concerned, it was directed by Peter Hall at the Arts Theatre, London in 1954, but has never been part of the repertoire of either of our national theatre companies. The great challenge which Lorca's play offers to British actors and directors in relation to the performance of its songs, its dances and its passionate poetry, has still to be taken up.

The source of *Blood Wedding* was an account in a Granada newspaper of an actual event: on 22 July 1928, in the Andalusian village of Nijar, Francisca Cañadas Morales was to marry Casimiro Pérez Morales, a young farmhand, but eloped with her cousin, Francisco Montes Cañadas, before the wedding could take place. Ambushed on the road by Francisca's sister and brother-in-law, who had arranged the marriage, Francisco Montes was murdered and Francisca left for dead, victims of a powerful mixture of greed, offended honour and vengeance, though the girl was to survive the attack and the murderers subsequently confessed their crime. Five years after the event, Lorca worked its essential details into the plot of his own play, but, that being so, was also influenced by many other factors. It is not insignificant, for example, that the composition of his own tragic trilogy, *Blood Wedding*, *Yerma* and *The House of Bernarda Alba*, should have coincided with spectacular outdoor performances in Barcelona, Madrid, Mérida and Salamanca of classical tragedies such as Seneca's *Medea*. From 1931 to 1935 Lorca was also the artistic director of the government-sponsored touring theatre company, *La Barraca*, with whom he produced many outstanding seventeenth-century Spanish 'classics': Lope de Vega's *The Sheep Well* and *The Knight of Olmedo* and Tirso de Molina's *The Trickster of Seville* among them. Another important influence was undoubtedly J.M. Synge's *Riders to the Sea* which Lorca knew well. It is a play in which, as in *Blood Wedding*, a mother's sons are taken from her, and it has too that dark vision of the world and a way of transforming characters and objects into more universal metaphors which came to distinguish Lorca's work. In this respect the symbolic realism of Ibsen must also be mentioned as a general influence, and so must Shakespeare, for Romeo and Juliet appear as characters in Lorca's *The Public*, and the family feud of Shakespeare's play has echoes in *Blood Wedding*. In the end, though, Lorca's vision of humanity's tragic helplessness in a hostile universe was a response to his own circumstances: society's victimization of 'outsiders', especially homosexuals; New York's appalling impassivity in the face of poverty and suffering, and his own increasing awareness of the gulf between reality and human aspiration. In his three tragedies, Lorca expressed in particular the clash between the individual who follows the path of instinct – in *Blood Wedding*, the Bride and Leonardo – and the forces of convention and tradition which stand in his or her way, a conflict of which he was only too keenly aware.

For all its apparent realism – source, setting and

characters – *Blood Wedding* is Lorca's most poetic play. In the first place the tendency of his earlier work to 'universalize' the characters is now very marked, for generic instead of real names give them an archetypal and symbolic quality: the Mother, the Father, the Bride, the Bridegroom, the Wife, the Neighbour, the Girl. Only the Bride's lover, Leonardo, has a real name, but even this is strongly symbolic, its first half suggesting the strength of a lion, its second the fire or passion (Spanish 'león' means 'lion', 'ardo' I burn'). Secondly, although the characters are individualized and differentiated, their experience is never merely their own. When, for example, the Mother laments the death of her husband and her elder son and expresses her fears for the younger, her grief and apprehension are quickly linked to the experience of other characters: in Scene One to the Neighbour's grief; in Scene Two to the isolation of the Wife; later on to the Bride's grief and the weeping of the neighbours. Furthermore, the human characters are constantly linked to the natural world – to the earth, flowers, crops, plants, water, animals, sun, cold – in a way which sets them in the greater context of Nature's inevitable rhythms, positive and negative, creative and destructive, and sharpens both a sense of human destiny and human helplessness. The Bride's attempt to explain her elopement with Leonardo is a very powerful statement indeed of her and others' inability to escape their fate: 'Your son was my ambition and I haven't deceived him, but the other one's arm dragged me like a wave from the sea, the butt of a mule, and would have always dragged me, always, always . . .' (Act III, Scene Two).

While Acts I and II focus on the human characters, albeit in the heightened way described above, Act III projects the action on to a higher poetic level. Here, in a scene that has its origins in the final act of *When Five Years Pass*, the three woodcutters and the figures of the Moon and Death appear on stage, and the unseen forces spoken of earlier – fate, destiny – assume a physical form and presence as they go about their deadly business. Lorca's stylized treatment of the episode serves to universalize it, but this is achieved too by the way in which we, the audience, are made to feel the icy coldness of death – especially through the figure of the Moon – and thus its relevance to ourselves. In one way the scene is strongly symbolist, for it evokes the mysteries that lie beyond human perception; in another it is surrealist, for the dark wood and its ghastly inhabitants may be seen as the 'exteriorizations' of the lovers' fears, as well as our own.

Lorca's own stage directions, far from being naturalistic, point to deliberate stylization. It is not, for example, the detail of the setting for Act I, Scene One, that should predominate in performance but the overall effect, the image of grief and foreboding created by the interaction of yellow walls, starkly suggested – *Room painted yellow*, the black of the women's dresses and the lack of physical movement for most of the scene. Lorca's love of stage-pictures whose resonances go beyond what is actually seen on stage characterizes the play as a whole, either developing the sense of fatality or, as in Act I, Scene Three, contrasting it with the optimism of the Bride's father's house with its *lace curtains and pink ribbon*. In short, stage settings should suggest those contrasts and tensions that lie at the very heart of the play – harmony/discord, grief/joy, aspiration/frustration, that build relentlessly towards the climax of the wedding celebrations, Act II, Scene Two, and dissolve into the pessimism of Act III.

Particularly important too in this respect, both here and in *Yerma*, is the play's music: its songs, poetry and poetic prose. It goes without saying that only in Spanish can Lorca's effects be fully realized and only then by actors with a knowledge of the traditional folk-music and dances of Andalusia. Thus, the lullaby of Act I, Scene Two, should capture the play's darkening mood and throw its shadow over the scenes that follow; the vibrant songs of the wedding scenes, enveloping the central characters, should dispel that darkness, like the sun the clouds, and the heavy monotonous intonation of the woodcutters should establish the final sense of inevitable tragedy. Not for nothing did Lorca's feeling for music reveal itself in his piano playing, his love of the guitar and his readings of his own plays and poetry.

Throughout *Blood Wedding* Lorca's instructions for the lighting of the stage should also be noted. As in all his theatre, lighting combines with other aspects of stage performance to reinforce the impact of key moments. So the wedding guests set off for the joyful ceremony as the sun rises and the stage is filled with light. So the darkness of the forest accompanies and intensifies the fears of the lovers, while the sudden invasion of the stage by an intense blue light, illuminating the white face of the moon, allows us to feel in our very bones the icy chill and menace of death. The brilliant combination of lighting, costume and poetry here is a perfect example of the theatrical style which Lorca devised in the 1930s with *La Barraca*, and which he simultaneously practised in his own plays.

III

Yerma, the second of the rural tragedies, quickly followed *Blood Wedding*, receiving its first performance at the Teatro Español in Madrid on 29 December 1934. The first-night audience, which packed the theatre, contained many distinguished people, but there were those too who resented Lorca's growing fame and others who objected to the friendship shown by the leading actress, Margarita

Xirgu, towards a former government minister, recently released from gaol. But early disruption of the performance quickly changed to rapt attention and admiration both for her performance and for Lorca's play. By the end it was a triumph, applauded by Enrique Diez-Canedo, literary critic and theatre reviewer for the Madrid newspaper, *La Voz*: 'We have a new poet-dramatist. Those who still doubted it . . . cannot deny it now. *Yerma* is the work of a poet, but not only of a poet . . . it is the work of a dramatic poet . . . In this tragic poem I see an action that gradually unfolds, with a protagonist and antagonist; but even if there were only the protagonist and the chorus, we would be in the presence of tragedy in its pure and ancient form . . .'

Condemned, like *Blood Wedding*, to years of subsequent neglect, *Yerma* burst dramatically on the world theatre scene again in the early seventies – ironically while Franco was still alive – in the controversial production of Victor Garcia. Taking the play's sub-title – *Tragic Poem in Three Acts and Six Scenes* – as his starting point, Garcia sought to express its poetic qualities through stylization of movement, action and song and, above all, by placing the action on a huge canvas trampoline that, lowered or raised at a given moment, could suggest either desert, valley, mountain or womb. This production, presented in London in 1973 as part of the World Theatre Season, was described by J.W. Lambert in *Drama* as 'obtrusive vulgarity' and by John Peter, in the same journal, as 'a self-indulgent and ostentatious piece of work' which 'used crude and haphazard physical symbolism where Lorca offers . . . only dark glimpses of the soul'. Such a reaction, indicative perhaps of excessive reverence for Lorca and of a failure to respond to full-blooded passion, should be set against the reception of Garcia's production, revived in Madrid in 1986 and recently seen at the Edinburgh Festival. Michael Ratcliffe, writing in the *Observer*, acknowledges both the universality of Lorca's play and the achievement of Victor García: 'The astounding design – an enormous grey trampoline slung inside a pentagonal steel ramp that thrusts out over the front stalls – is pulled by hawsers into a rolling landscape through which the fertile women of the village tread in triumph like horses, or into a steep precipice of the writhing damned.

'At the end of the play it collapses and withers into a dark sleeve of oblivion which pulls Yerma and the husband she has strangled into the earth like trash. García and Espert [Nuria Espert] take Lorca far beyond the confines of Spain, linking him with his precursors in the north and west, and Yerma herself with the wasted unlived lives in *Hedda Gabler* and *The Playboy of the Western World*.' This recognition of the poetic and universal quality of Lorca's theatre is exactly right.

In terms of its themes – especially longing and frustration – *Yerma* has much in common with *Blood Wedding*, but the tragedy of a family is now the tragedy of a single woman beside whose suffering the other characters seem almost insignificant. Trapped in a loveless marriage to the farmer, Juan, who takes more interest in his fields than in the child his wife longs for, Yerma is trapped too by social attitudes and conventions. On the one hand, the childless wife is an easy target for the mockery and scorn of village women for whom childbearing is the most natural thing in the world. On the other, although Yerma is drawn instinctively to another man, Victor, she is prevented from taking him as a lover both by her own conscience and by the social conventions of honour. Driven to a growing realization of the pointlessness of her life without a child, Yerma ensures that empty future by murdering her husband.

In contrast to *Blood Wedding*, *Yerma* has neither the heightened poetic symbolism of that play's final act nor the same amount of poetry. According to his brother,

Lorca believed that his theatre would benefit from a greater austerity and fewer lyric elements, and *Yerma* does indeed have only seven examples of poetry, all of them songs, five of them short and sung by Yerma herself. But to regard this as an indication of the play's greater 'naturalism' would be quite wrong.

Once more the characters' names have an archetypal ring. Yerma itself is not, in fact, a real name but an adjective meaning 'barren', 'empty', 'bare', 'uninhabited', which is normally applied to the land and which, used in relation to the play's protagonist, describes not so much the woman as the state of physical and emotional emptiness which is her lot and, by extension, the lot of other women like her. The two men, admittedly, have real names – Juan and Victor – but otherwise embody virility, in Victor's case, or its opposite, in Juan's. And, grouped around the central trio, the other characters personify to a greater or lesser degree the fertility which they have, aspire to, or lack: the Old Woman, the First Girl, the six village women, the Male, the Female. In addition, the human characters are firmly placed in the context of Nature seen as part of it, and related to the cycles of birth, death, fertility and barrenness that are part of the natural world. As in *Blood Wedding*, the interweaving of Man and Nature invests the characters and events of the play with a truly universal and even mythical significance.

The poetic and symbolic thrust of *Yerma* may be gauged, too, by Lorca's indications for its staging. In his stage directions for physical locations, there is a notable starkness and lack of realistic detail. Thus, Scene One is set in Yerma's house, but the stage direction has no description of a room, only a reference to an embroidery frame: *When the curtain rises, Yerma is asleep, an embroidery frame at her feet*. Attention is focused only on an object which represents the inescapable reality of her domestic tasks and thus the traditional nature of her role. Later, in Act II, Scene Two, stage directions draw attention to the door of the house which Juan has instructed must now be closed and which, therefore, signposts Yerma's growing sense of imprisonment. Similarly, pitchers brimming with water are a mocking reminder of Yerma's sterility, while the settings for outdoor scenes, all reduced to the very minimum of detail, evoke the freedom and space which are slowly denied her. In short, Lorca's intention was to pinpoint only those elements of staging which he considered significant in relation to Yerma's emotional and psychological life.

The lighting of the stage has the same function. At the outset it is brightly lit, corresponding to Yerma's hopeful dream of a child. As her hopes slowly fade, the scenes move into twilight – Act II, Scene Two – and then darkness. In contrast, the episodes in the fields and at the stream – Act II, Scene One – are full of sunlight, the physical counterpart of the joy and vitality of the village women as a whole. The visual patterns of the play – and these involve movement too – can be seen as emotional graphs designed to plot its evolving pattern and to draw the audience along with it.

Finally, the play's stylization can be noted in its patterned and structured dialogue. Yerma and Juan are people obsessed – Juan by land and profit, Yerma by the need for a child – and their words revolve constantly around those issues, rarely touching on anything else. The dialogue is repetitive, concentrated, stripped of extraneous matters and, as the play unfolds, it is more and more concerned with Yerma's uselessness, ugliness, worthlessness and – in her own eyes – badness. The range is narrow, a closed circle of language whose pattern reflects the way in which, emotionally, she turns in on herself. In contrast, the gossip and songs of the village women at the stream are expansive and vibrant, the rhythms springy, the images replete with life and colour. In a sense it is possible to talk of the play's language in terms of a piece of music in which a passage in the minor key is suddenly transposed to the major – bright, dazzling, inspiring – before returning again to the minor. But there is more than that to it in Lorca's play, for the language is but a single element in a unified composition of stage setting, movement, lighting, song and speech in which each reinforces the other and none can be considered in total isolation.

IV

Doña Rosita the Spinster was completed in June 1935 and received its triumphant première in December of that year at the Teatro Principal Palace in Barcelona. Less well known than the three tragedies, it is a supremely accomplished piece. Lorca himself observed that the play had already been written in his mind in 1924 when a friend told him the story of a mutable rose, described in a seventeenth-century book about roses. According to his brother, Francisco, the public success of *Mariana Pineda* in 1927 had done little to compensate a private sense of failure and dissatisfaction with the play, a feeling that was finally overcome with the composition of *Doña Rosita* eight years later. Like the earlier play, it is concerned with a woman who waits in vain for her lover's return, though it lacks *Mariana Pineda*'s political dimension, and it is set too in Lorca's beloved Granada. Thematically there are links with *When Five Years Pass* where passing time and love's frustration figure prominently, and also, of course, with *Yerma*. Like Yerma, Rosita advances from hope to a growing sense of isolation, but she is Yerma in another key, more muted and restrained, and although the play's sadness frequently moves one to tears, it is offset by the most delightful comic moments. In *Doña Rosita* Lorca is, in fact, not unlike Chekhov. At the end of the play the famiy leaves the house it has lived in for many years to the sound of a door banging in the wind. Comparisons with *The Cherry Orchard* are inevitable, and Lorca's play has in abundance Chekhov's characteristic mixture of laughter and tears. But no one with any knowledge of Lorca's theatre could fail to recognize how truly Lorquian *Doña Rosita* is in its themes, its poetry and its anguished portrayal of the central character.

In terms of dramatic technique, the play looks back to *Yerma* and *Blood Wedding* and forward to *The House of Bernarda Alba*, for on the one hand it is distinguished by passages of poetry, often extremely lyrical, and on the other by a greater degree of realism. Directions for the costumes of the characters are, for example, precise and detailed, and locate them firmly in a specific period of time. Such is the case when Rosita first enters: *She wears a rose-coloured dress, in the style of 1900, with leg-of-mutton sleeves and trimmed with braid*. Again, when the three spinsters and their mother appear in Act II, the stage direction reads: *The* THREE SPINSTERS *wear huge hats with tasteless feathers, ridiculous dresses, gloves to the elbow with bracelets over them, and fans dangling from long chains. The* MOTHER *wears a faded black dress and a hat with old purple ribbons*. A consideration of the dialogue also points to a greater realism, for it is frequently concerned with the everyday affairs of Rosita and her family, be it the Uncle's obsession with his flowers, the Housekeeper's gossip, or the young women's chatter about current taste and fashion. Conversations of this kind, desultory and often commonplace, occur much more often in this play than in either *Yerma* or *Blood Wedding*, and it is not therefore difficult to understand why *Doña Rosita* has often been regarded as more naturalistic.

But it is a view of the play which requires qualification.

The apparent naturalism of sets and costumes is in actual fact a piece of highly effective stylization, for each individual act presents a picture and the three acts together a succession of images of passing time and inevitable change. It is a symbolism caught above all in the key association of Rosita's costume, changing through the play from red to pink to white, and the mutable rose that at noon is red, by evening pink, by nightfall white and dead. The play as a whole is thus a metaphor of life's passing, of dreams and disillusionment, and of human fragility. Moreover, close consideration of the dialogue suggests that even if it seems to dwell on day-to-day affairs, these are invariably part of the play's central themes and, inasmuch as they preoccupy the characters, have precisely that obsessive quality that is so characteristic of the tragedies themselves. The seeming naturalness of the dialogue conceals an artfulness which is as great here as in any of the major plays, and by Act III, where Rosita's despair is fully borne in on her, the expression of her feelings in repeated phrases and insistent rhythms links her very firmly to Yerma:

> One day a friend gets married, and then another, and yet another, and the next day she has a son, and the son grows up and comes to show me his examination marks. Or there are new houses and new songs. And there am I, with the same trembling excitement, cutting the same carnations, looking at the same clouds . . .

The fact that Rosita makes us think of Yerma indicates, moreover, that while she is a strongly delineated individual, she is also part of that long line of despairing and abandoned women who fill Lorca's plays and poems.

Above all, the play's symbolic resonances spring from its

poetry and, in particular, the poem about the mutable rose. Highly effective in itself, the poem's effectiveness is doubled through its haunting relevance to and implications for Rosita as she grows progressively older. In this respect the ending of the play is quite magical, for Rosita, pale, dressed in white, almost fainting with emotion, is the rose at the end of its life, and, as she walks out into the darkness of night, the white curtains fluttering in the wind become the rose's falling petals. The central image of the poem has become, in a quite brilliant and evocative moment, the entire stage-picture, the naturalistic moments of the play transformed into a final, breathtaking piece of symbolism.

Gwynne Edwards, 1987

Blood Wedding

Translated by Gwynne Edwards

This translation of *Blood Wedding* was first performed at the Contact theatre, Manchester on 11 November 1987, with the following cast:

THE MOTHER	Maureen Morris
THE BRIDE	Sara Mair Thomas
THE MOTHER-IN-LAW/GIRL 2	Anni Domingo
THE NEIGHBOUR/THE SERVANT	Fenella Norman
THE WIFE OF LEONARDO	Charlotte Harvey
GIRL 1/DEATH (as a beggar woman)	Joan Carol Williams
LEONARDO	Tyrone Huggins
THE BRIDEGROOM	Ewen Cummins
THE FATHER OF THE BRIDE/THE MOON	Wyllie Longmore
YOUTH	Mark Crowshaw

WOODCUTTERS/GIRLS/GUESTS played by members of the Company

Directed by Anthony Clark
Designed by Nettie Edwards
Musical Director/Composer Mark Vibrans
Lighting by Stephen Henbest
Choreography by David Needham

Act One

Room painted yellow.

BRIDEGROOM (*entering*). Mother.

MOTHER. What?

BRIDEGROOM. I'm going.

MOTHER. Where to?

BRIDEGROOM. To the vineyard. (*He starts to go out.*)

MOTHER. Wait.

BRIDEGROOM. Do you want something?

MOTHER. Son, your breakfast.

BRIDEGROOM. Leave it. I'll eat grapes. Give me the knife.

MOTHER. What for?

BRIDEGROOM (*laughing*). To cut them.

MOTHER (*muttering and looking for it*). The knife, the knife ... Damn all of them and the scoundrel who invented them.

BRIDEGROOM. Let's change the subject.

MOTHER. And shotguns . . and pistols ... even the tiniest knife ... and mattocks and pitchforks ...

BRIDEGROOM. Alright.

MOTHER. Everything that can cut a man's body. A beautiful man, tasting the fullness of life, who goes out to the vineyards or tends to his olives, because they are his, inherited ...

BRIDEGROOM (*lowering his head*). Be quiet.

33

MOTHER. . . . and that man doesn't come back. Or if he does come back it's to put a palm-leaf on him or a plateful of coarse salt to stop him swelling. I don't know how you dare carry a knife on your body, nor how I can leave the serpent inside the chest.

BRIDEGROOM. Is that it?

MOTHER. If I lived to be a hundred, I wouldn't speak of anything else. First your father. He had the scent of carnation for me, and I enjoyed him for three short years. Then your brother. Is it fair? Is it possible that a thing as small as a pistol or a knife can put an end to a man who's a bull? I'll never be quiet. The months pass and hopelessness pecks at my eyes . . . even at the roots of my hair.

BRIDEGROOM (*forcefully*). Are you going to stop?

MOTHER. No. I won't stop. Can someone bring your father back to me? And your brother? And then there's the gaol. What is the gaol? They eat there, they smoke there, they play instruments there. My dead ones full of weeds, silent, turned to dust; two men who were two geraniums . . . The murderers, in gaol, as large as life, looking at the mountains . . .

BRIDEGROOM. Do you want me to kill them?

MOTHER. No . . . If I speak it's because . . . How am I not going to speak seeing you go out of that door? I don't like you carrying a knife. It's just that . . . I wish you wouldn't go out to the fields.

BRIDEGROOM (*laughing*). Come on!

MOTHER. I'd like you to be a woman. You wouldn't be going to the stream now and the two of us would embroider edgings and little woollen dogs.

BRIDEGROOM (*he puts his arm around his mother and laughs*). Mother, what if I were to take you with me to the vineyards?

MOTHER. What would an old woman do in the

vineyards? Would you put me under the vine-shoots?

BRIDEGROOM (*lifting her in his arms*). You old woman, you old, old woman, you old, old, old woman.

MOTHER. Your father, now he used to take me there. That's good stock. Good blood. Your grandfather left a son on every street corner. That's what I like. Men to be men; wheat wheat.

BRIDEGROOM. What about me, mother?

MOTHER. You? What?

BRIDEGROOM. Do I need to tell you again?

MOTHER (*serious*). Ah!

BRIDEGROOM. Do you think it's a bad idea?

MOTHER. No.

BRIDEGROOM. Well then?

MOTHER. I'm not sure. It's so sudden like this. It's taken me by surprise. I know that the girl's good. She is, isn't she? Well-behaved. Hard-working. She makes her bread and she sews her skirts. But even so, when I mention her name, it's as if they were pounding my head with a stone.

BRIDEGROOM. Don't be silly.

MOTHER. It's more than silly. I'll be left alone. Only you are left to me now and I'm sorry to see you going.

BRIDEGROOM. But you'll come with us.

MOTHER. No. I can't leave your father and your brother here. I have to go to them every morning, and if I leave, one of the Felixes could die, one of the family of murderers, and they'd bury him next to mine. I won't stand for that. Never that! Because I'll dig them up with my nails and all on my own I'll smash them to bits against the wall.

BRIDEGROOM (*strongly*). Back to that again!

MOTHER. I'm sorry. (*Pause.*) How long have you known her?

BRIDEGROOM. Three years. And now I've bought

the vineyard.

MOTHER. Three years. She had another young man, didn't she?

BRIDEGROOM. I don't know. I don't think so. Girls have to be careful who they marry.

MOTHER. Yes. I didn't look at anyone else. I looked at your father, and when they killed him I stared at the wall in front of me. One woman with one man, and there it is.

BRIDEGROOM. You know that my girl's good.

MOTHER. I don't doubt it. All the same, I'd like to know what her mother was like.

BRIDEGROOM. What's it matter?

MOTHER (*looking at him*). Son.

BRIDEGROOM. What do you want?

MOTHER. It's true. You're right. When do you want me to ask for her?

BRIDEGROOM (*happy*). Does Sunday seem alright?

MOTHER (*serious*). I'll take her the brass earrings, the really old ones, and you buy her . . .

BRIDEGROOM. But you know more . . .

MOTHER. You buy her some patterned stockings, and for yourself two suits . . . No. Three! I've only got you!

BRIDEGROOM. I'm going. I'll go and see her tomorrow.

MOTHER. Yes, yes, and see if you can make me happy with six grandchildren, or as many as you want, seeing your father didn't have a chance to give them to me.

BRIDEGROOM. The first one for you.

MOTHER. Yes, but let them be girls. Because I want to embroider and make lace and be at peace.

BRIDEGROOM. I'm sure you'll love my bride.

MOTHER. I will. (*She goes to kiss him but stops.*) Go on. You are far too big for kisses now. Give them to your wife. (*Pause. Aside.*) When she is your wife.

BRIDEGROOM. I'm going.

MOTHER. Dig the land by the little mill. You've been neglecting it.

BRIDEGROOM. It's settled then.

MOTHER. God go with you.

The BRIDEGROOM *leaves. The* MOTHER *remains seated, with her back to the door. A* NEIGHBOUR *appears at the door dressed in dark colours, a handkerchief on her head.*

Come in.

NEIGHBOUR. How are you?

MOTHER. You can see for yourself.

NEIGHBOUR. I came down to the shop so I've come to see you. We live so far from each other.

MOTHER. It's twenty years since I went to the top of the street.

NEIGHBOUR. You look well.

MOTHER. You think so?

NEIGHBOUR. Things happen. Two days ago they brought my neighbour's son home . . . both arms cut clean off by the machine. (*She sits down.*)

MOTHER. Rafael?

NEIGHBOUR. Yes. There it is. I often think your son and mine are better off where they are, sleeping, resting, no chance of being crippled.

MOTHER. Be quiet. It's all talk that, but there's no comfort in it.

They both sigh. Pause.

NEIGHBOUR (*sadly*). How is your son?

MOTHER. He's gone out.

NEIGHBOUR. He's bought the vineyard then!

MOTHER. He was lucky.

NEIGHBOUR. He'll get married now.

MOTHER (*as though waking up and drawing her chair to the* NEIGHBOUR'*s chair*). Listen.

NEIGHBOUR (*in a conspiratorial manner*). What is it?

MOTHER. Do you know my son's sweetheart?

NEIGHBOUR. A good girl!

MOTHER. Yes, but . . .

NEIGHBOUR. But there's no one knows her really well. She lives alone with her father out there, it's so far away, ten leagues from the nearest house. But she is good. She's used to solitude.

MOTHER. What about her mother?

NEIGHBOUR. Her mother, now I did know her. A good-looking woman. A glow on her face like a saint's; but I never liked her. She didn't love her husband.

MOTHER (*strongly*). Well, the things people get to know!

NEIGHBOUR. I'm sorry. I didn't mean to offend; but it's true. Now if she was respectable or not, no one ever said. No one ever mentioned that. She was proud.

MOTHER. It's always the same!

NEIGHBOUR. You did ask me.

MOTHER. I wish no one knew either of them – the girl or her mother. That they were like two thistles that no one dares name, and if you do they prick you.

NEIGHBOUR. You're right. Your son's precious.

MOTHER. He is. That's why I take care of him. They told me the girl had a young man some time ago.

NEIGHBOUR. She must have been fifteen. He got married two years ago now, to a cousin of hers in fact. No one remembers the engagement.

MOTHER. Why do you remember?

NEIGHBOUR. You do ask some questions!

MOTHER. Everyone likes to know about the things that hurt them. Who was the boy?

NEIGHBOUR. Leonardo.

MOTHER. Which Leonardo?

NEIGHBOUR. Leonardo, one of the Félix family.

MOTHER (*getting up*). The Félix family!

NEIGHBOUR. Woman, how can Leonardo be blamed

for anything? He was eight years old when those things happened.

MOTHER. I know . . . But I hear that name – Félix – and for me Félix is the same as filling my mouth with slime (*She spits.*) and I have to spit, I have to spit so it doesn't poison me.

NEIGHBOUR. Calm down. What good does it do you?

MOTHER. None. But you understand.

NEIGHBOUR. Don't stand in the way of your son's happiness. Don't tell him anything. You're an old woman. Me too. You and me, we have to keep quiet.

MOTHER. I won't say anything.

NEIGHBOUR (*kissing her*). Nothing.

MOTHER (*calmly*). Things! . . .

NEIGHBOUR. I'm going. My family will be back soon from the fields.

MOTHER. Have you ever seen such a hot day?

NEIGHBOUR. The children were fed up taking water to the harvesters. God be with you, woman.

MOTHER. God be with you.

The MOTHER *moves towards the door stage-left. Half-way there she stops and slowly crosses herself.*

Scene Two

A room painted pink, with copper ornaments and bunches of common flowers. Centre-stage, a table with a cloth. It is morning. LEONARDO'S MOTHER-IN-LAW *with a child in her arms. She rocks it. The* WIFE, *in the other corner, is knitting.*

MOTHER-IN-LAW. Lullaby, my baby sweet,
  Of the great big stallion
  Wouldn't drink the water deep.

There the water's oh so black,
Where the trees grow thick and strong.
When it flows down to the bridge,
There it stops and sings its song.

Who can say, my little one,
What the water's anguish is,
As he draws his tail along,
Through that nice green room of his.

WIFE (*quietly*). Go to sleep, carnation,
For the horse will not drink deep.
MOTHER-IN-LAW. Go to sleep, my little rose,
For the horse now starts to weep.

Horsey's hooves are red with blood,
Horsey's mane is frozen,
Deep inside his staring eyes
A silver dagger broken.

Down they went to the river bank,
Down to the stream they rode.
There his blood ran strong and fast,
Faster than the water could.

WIFE. Go to sleep, carnation,
For the horse will not drink deep.
MOTHER-IN-LAW. Go to sleep, my little rose,
For the horse now starts to weep.
WIFE. Horsey will not touch the bank,
Even though the bank is wet,
Even though his mouth is hot,
Streaming tiny drops of sweat.

To the mountains cold and hard,
He could only call and neigh,
Horsey's throat is hot and parched,
And the river bed is dry.

Oh, the great big stallion,
Wouldn't drink the water deep,
Pain as sharp as coldest ice,
Horse at break of day will weep.

MOTHER-IN-LAW. Don't come near. Stay outside.
Close the window, close it tight.
Weave a branch of finest dream,
Dream a branch so fine and light.

WIFE. Now my child is sleeping fast.

MOTHER-IN-LAW. Now my child will rest at last.

WIFE. Horsey, I would have you know,
Baby has a nice soft pillow.

MOTHER-IN-LAW. Baby's cradle made of steel.

WIFE. Baby's quilt so fine to feel.

MOTHER-IN-LAW. Lullaby, my baby sweet.

WIFE. Oh, the great big stallion,
Wouldn't drink the water deep.

MOTHER-IN-LAW. Don't come near, don't come in.
Seek the far off mountain.
Find the dark, the grey valley,
There the mare will waiting be.

WIFE (*looking*). Now my child is sleeping fast.

MOTHER-IN-LAW. Now my child will rest at last.

WIFE (*quietly*). Go to sleep, carnation,
For the horse will not drink deep.

MOTHER-IN-LAW (*rising and very quietly*).
Go to sleep, my little rose,
For the horse now starts to weep.

They take the child out. LEONARDO *enters.*

LEONARDO. Where's the baby?

WIFE. Fast asleep.

LEONARDO. He wasn't well yesterday. He cried in
the night.

WIFE (*happy*). He's like a dahlia today. What about you?

Did you go to the blacksmith's?

LEONARDO. That's where I've come from. Would you believe? More than two months putting new shoes on the horse, and they always come off him. I reckon he rips them off on the stones.

WIFE. Couldn't it be you ride him a lot?

LEONARDO. No. I hardly ever ride him.

WIFE. Yesterday the neighbours told me they'd seen you the other side of the plains.

LEONARDO. Who said that?

WIFE. The women who pick capers. It surprised me, I can tell you. Was it you?

LEONARDO. No. What would I be doing over there, in that dry place?

WIFE. That's what I said. But the horse was half dead from sweating.

LEONARDO. Did you see him?

WIFE. No. My mother.

LEONARDO. Is she with the baby?

WIFE. Yes. Do you want a drink of lemon?

LEONARDO. With the water really cold.

WIFE. Not coming back to eat!

LEONARDO. I was with the wheat-weighers. They always hold people up.

WIFE (*making the drink, softly*). Do they pay a good price?

LEONARDO. Average.

WIFE. I need a dress. The baby needs a cap with ribbons.

LEONARDO (*getting up*). I'm going to see him.

WIFE. Take care. He's asleep.

MOTHER-IN-LAW (*entering*). So who's racing the horse like that? He's down there stretched out with his eyes bulging as if he's come from the end of the world.

LEONARDO (*sharply*). Me.

MOTHER-IN-LAW. Excuse me, he is yours.

WIFE (*timidly*). He was with the wheat-weighers.

MOTHER-IN-LAW. For all I care, he can burst. (*She sits down. Pause.*)

WIFE. The drink. Is it cold enough?

LEONARDO. Yes.

WIFE. Do you know they're asking for my cousin?

LEONARDO. When?

WIFE. Tomorrow. The wedding will be in less than a month. I expect they'll invite us.

LEONARDO (*seriously*). I don't know.

MOTHER-IN-LAW. I don't think his mother was very happy about the wedding.

LEONARDO. Perhaps she's right. That one needs watching.

WIFE. I don't like you thinking bad things about a good girl.

MOTHER-IN-LAW (*with malice*). When he says that it's because he knows her. Don't you know she was his girl for three years?

LEONARDO. But I left her. (*To his* WIFE.) Are you going to cry now? Stop it! (*He roughly pulls her hands from her face.*) Let's go and see the child.

They go out with their arms around each other. A GIRL *enters. She runs on happily.*

GIRL. Señora.

MOTHER-IN-LAW. What is it?

GIRL. The young man came to the shop and he bought all the best things.

MOTHER-IN-LAW. Was he alone?

GIRL. No. With his mother. Serious, tall. (*She imitates her.*) But very posh.

MOTHER-IN-LAW. They've got money.

GIRL. And they bought these fancy stockings! You should have seen them! The stockings women dream of! Look: a swallow here (*She points to her ankle.*), a boat there (*She points to her calf.*), and here a rose. (*She points to her thigh.*)

MOTHER-IN-LAW. Child!

GIRL. A rose with the seeds and the stalk! And all in silk!

MOTHER-IN-LAW. Two fortunes joined together.

LEONARDO *and his* WIFE *enter.*

GIRL. I've come to tell you what they're buying.

LEONARDO (*angrily*). We couldn't care less.

WIFE. Leave her.

MOTHER-IN-LAW. Leonardo, there's no need for that.

GIRL. Excuse me. (*She goes out weeping.*)

MOTHER-IN-LAW. Why do you have to upset people?

LEONARDO. I didn't ask for your opinion. (*He sits down.*)

MOTHER-IN-LAW. Very well. (*Pause.*)

WIFE (*to* LEONARDO). What's the matter with you? What's boiling away inside your head? Don't leave me like this, not knowing anything . . .

LEONARDO. Stop it!

WIFE. No. I want you to look at me and tell me.

LEONARDO. Leave me alone. (*He gets up.*)

WIFE. Where are you going?

LEONARDO (*sharply*). Can't you shut up?

MOTHER-IN-LAW (*forcefully, to her daughter*). Be quiet! (LEONARDO *leaves.*) The baby.

She goes out and reappears with the child in her arms. The WIFE *is still standing, motionless.*

Horsey's hooves are red with blood.
Horsey's mane is frozen.
Deep inside his staring eyes
A silver dagger broken.
Down they went to the river bank,
Down to the stream they rode.

There his blood ran strong and fast,
Faster than the water could.
WIFE (*turning slowly, as if in a dream*).
Go to sleep, carnation,
For the horse will now drink deep.
MOTHER-IN-LAW. Go to sleep, my little rose,
For the horse now starts to weep.
WIFE. Lullaby, my baby sweet.
MOTHER-IN-LAW. Oh, the great big stallion,
Wouldn't drink the water deep!
WIFE (*strongly*). Don't come near, don't come in.
Go away to the far-off mountain.
Oh, the pain is sharp as ice,
Horse of dawn that's breaking.
MOTHER-IN-LAW (*weeping*).
Now my child is sleeping fast.
WIFE (*weeping and slowly drawing closer*).
Now my child will rest at last.
MOTHER-IN-LAW. Go to sleep carnation,
For the horse will not drink deep.
WIFE (*weeping and leaning on the table*).
Go to sleep, my little rose,
For the horse now starts to weep.

Curtain

Scene Three

Interior of the cave where the BRIDE *lives. At the back a cross of big pink flowers. The doors are round with lace curtains and pink ribbon. On the walls, made of a white hard material, are round fans, blue jars and small mirrors.*

SERVANT. Please come in . . . (*She is pleasant, hypocritically deferential.*)

The BRIDEGROOM *and the* MOTHER *enter. The* MOTHER *is dressed in black satin and wears a lace mantilla. The* BRIDEGROOM *in black corduroy, wearing a chain of gold.*

Would you like to sit down? They'll be here soon.

She goes out. The MOTHER *and the* BRIDEGROOM *remain seated, stiff as statues. A long pause.*

MOTHER. Have you got your watch?

BRIDEGROOM. Yes. (*He takes it out and looks at it.*)

MOTHER. We have to get back in good time. These people live so far away!

BRIDEGROOM. But this land's good.

MOTHER. Yes, but too isolated. Four hours' journey and not a house or tree.

BRIDEGROOM. These are the dry lands.

MOTHER. Your father would have covered them with trees.

BRIDEGROOM. Without water?

MOTHER. He'd have looked for it. The three years he was married to me, he planted ten cherry trees. (*Recalling.*) Three walnut trees by the mill, a whole vineyard and a plant called Jupiter that has red flowers. But it dried up. (*Pause.*)

BRIDEGROOM (*referring to the* BRIDE). She must be getting dressed.

The FATHER *of the* BRIDE *enters, an old man with shining white hair. His head is bowed. The* MOTHER *and the* BRIDEGROOM *rise and they shake hands in silence.*

FATHER. Did the journey take long?

MOTHERFour hours. (*They sit down.*)

FATHER. You must have come the longest way round.

MOTHER. I'm too old to cross the rough ground by the river.

BRIDEGROOM. It makes her giddy. (*Pause.*)

FATHER. A good crop of esparto.

BRIDEGROOM. Oh, very good.

FATHER. In my day this land didn't even produce esparto. I've had to punish it, even make it suffer, so it gives us something useful.

MOTHER. And now it does. Don't worry. I'm not going to ask you for anything.

FATHER (*smiling*). You are better off than me. Your vineyards are worth a fortune. Each vine-shoot a silver coin. What I'm sorry about is that the estates are . . . you know . . . separate. I like everything together. There's just one thorn in my heart, and that's that little orchard stuck between my fields, and they won't sell it to me for all the gold in the world.

BRIDEGROOM. It's always the same.

FATHER. If we could use twenty teams of oxen to bring your vineyards here and put them on the hillside. What a joy it would be!

MOTHER. But why?

FATHER. Mine is hers and yours his. That's why. To see it all together. Together, that would be a thing of beauty!

BRIDEGROOM. And it would be less work.

MOTHER. When I die, you can sell that and buy here next to this.

FATHER. Sell, sell! No! Buy, woman, buy everything. If I'd had sons, I'd have bought the whole of this hill right up to the stream. It's not good land; but with your arms you can make it good, and since no one passes by they don't steal the fruit and you can sleep easy. (*Pause.*)

MOTHER. You know why I've come.

FATHER. Yes.

MOTHER. So?

FATHER. I approve. They've talked it over.

MOTHER. My son has plenty, and he knows how to manage it.

FATHER. My daughter too.

MOTHER. My son's handsome. He's never known a woman. His name's cleaner than a sheet spread in the sun.

FATHER. What can I tell you about my girl? She's breaking up bread at three when the morning star's shining. She never talks too much; she's as soft as wool; she does all kinds of embroidery, and she can cut a piece of string with her teeth.

MOTHER. May God bless their house.

FATHER. May God bless it.

> *The* SERVANT *appears with two trays. One with glasses and the other with sweets.*

MOTHER (*to the* SON). When would you like the wedding to be?

BRIDEGROOM. Next Thursday.

FATHER. The same day as her twenty-second birthday.

MOTHER. Twenty-two. That's what my son would have been if he were still alive. He'd be alive, warm, the true man that he was, if men hadn't invented knives.

FATHER. You mustn't dwell on that.

MOTHER. Every minute. Put your hand on your heart.

FATHER. Thursday then. Agreed?

BRIDEGROOM. Agreed.

FATHER. The bride and groom and we two, we'll go to the church in a carriage. It's a very long way. And the guests in the carts and on the horses they bring with them.

MOTHER. Agreed.

> *The* SERVANT *comes in.*

FATHER. Tell her to come in now. (*To the* MOTHER.) I'll be very happy if you like her.

> *The* BRIDE *enters. Her hands at her sides in a modest pose, her head bowed.*

MOTHER. Come! Are you happy?

BRIDE. Yes, señora.

FATHER. You mustn't be so serious. After all, she's going to be your mother.

BRIDE. I'm happy. When I say 'yes' it's because I want to.

MOTHER. Of course. (*She takes her by the chin.*) Look at me.

FATHER. She's like my wife in every way.

MOTHER. Is she? Such a lovely expression! You know what getting married is, child?

BRIDE (*solemnly*). I do.

MOTHER. A man, children, and as for the rest a wall that's two feet thick.

BRIDEGROOM. Who needs anything else?

MOTHER. Only that they should live. That's all . . . that they should live!

BRIDE. I know my duty.

MOTHER. Some gifts for you.

BRIDE. Thank you.

FATHER. Will you take something?

MOTHER. I'd rather not. (*To the* BRIDEGROOM.) Will you?

BRIDEGROOM. I will. (*He takes a sweetmeat. The* BRIDE *takes another.*)

FATHER (*to the* BRIDEGROOM.) Wine?

MOTHER. He doesn't touch it.

FATHER. That's good! (*Pause. They are all standing.*)

BRIDEGROOM (to the BRIDE.) I'll come tomorrow.

BRIDE. At what time?

BRIDEGROOM. At five.

BRIDE. I'll expect you.

BRIDE. When I leave your side I feel a great emptiness and a kind of lump in my throat.

BRIDE. When you are my husband you won't have it any more.

BRIDEGROOM. That's what I keep telling myself.

MOTHER. Let's go then. The sun doesn't wait. (*To the* FATHER.) Are we agreed on everything?

FATHER. Agreed.

MOTHER (*to the* SERVANT). Goodbye, woman.

SERVANT. God go with both of you.

The MOTHER *kisses the* BRIDE *and they begin to leave quietly.*

MOTHER (*at the door*). Goodbye, daughter.

The BRIDE *replies with a gesture.*

FATHER. I'll come outside with you.

They go out.

SERVANT. I'm bursting to see the presents.

BRIDE (*harshly*). Stop it!

SERVANT. Child! Show them to me!

BRIDE. I don't want to.

SERVANT. Just the stockings then. They say they're very fancy. Woman!

BRIDE. I said no.

SERVANT. For God's sake! Alright. It's as if you have no wish to get married.

BRIDE (*biting her hand in anger*). Oh!

SERVANT. Child, child! What's the matter? Are you sorry to be giving up this queen's life? Don't think of bitter things. There's no reason. None. Let's see the presents. (*She takes the box.*)

BRIDE (*gripping her by the wrists*). Let go.

SERVANT. Woman!

BRIDE. Let go, I said.

SERVANT. You're stronger than a man.

BRIDE. Haven't I done a man's work? I wish I was one.

SERVANT. Don't talk like that!

BRIDE. Shut up, I said. Let's talk about something else.

The light begins to fade. A long pause.

SERVANT. Did you hear a horse last night?

BRIDE. What time?

SERVANT. Three o'clock.

BRIDE. Probably a horse strayed from the herd.

SERVANT. No. It had a rider.

BRIDE. How do you know?

SERVANT. Because I saw him. He was standing by your window. It gave me a start.

BRIDE. Probably my young man. He's been here sometimes at that time.

SERVANT. No.

BRIDE. You saw him?

SERVANT. Yes.

BRIDE. Who was it?

SERVANT. It was Leonardo.

BRIDE (*forcefully*). That's a lie! A lie! Why should he come here?

SERVANT. He *was* here.

BRIDE. Be quiet! Damn your tongue.

The sound of a horse is heard.

SERVANT (*at the window*). Look! Come here! Was it him?

BRIDE. Yes, it was.

Quick curtain.

Act Two

Scene One

Entrance to the BRIDE's *house. A large door in the background.
Night. The* BRIDE *enters dressed in a white ruffled petticoat with
lots of lace and embroidered edgings, and a white bodice. Her arms
are bare. The* SERVANT *is similarly dressed.*

SERVANT. I'll finish combing your hair out here.
BRIDE. No one can stay inside there in this heat.
SERVANT. In these lands it doesn't get cool even at dawn.

> *The* BRIDE *sits down on a low chair and looks at herself in a
> small hand-mirror. The* SERVANT *combs her hair.*

BRIDE. My mother came from a place where there were
  lots of trees. From a fertile land.
SERVANT. That's why she was full of joy.
BRIDE. She wasted away here.
SERVANT. Her fate.
BRIDE. Like we're all wasting away. The walls throw the
  heat out at us. Oh! Don't pull so hard.
SERVANT. It's to arrange this strand of hair better. I want
  it to come down over your forehead. (*The* BRIDE *looks at
  herself in the mirror.*) You do look beautiful! (*She kisses her
  with feeling.*)

BRIDE (*solemnly*). Just comb my hair.
SERVANT (*combing*). Such a lucky girl . . . to be able to put
  your arms around a man, to kiss him, to feel his
  weight!
BRIDE. Be quiet!
SERVANT. But it's best of all when you wake up and you
  feel him alongside you, and he strokes your shoulders
  with his breath, like a nightingale's feather.

52

BRIDE (*forcefully*). Will you be quiet!

SERVANT. But child! What is marriage? That's what marriage is. Nothing more! Is it the sweetmeats? Is it the bunches of flowers? Of course it's not! It's a shining bed and a man and a woman.

BRIDE. You shouldn't talk about such things.

SERVANT. That's another matter. But there's plenty of pleasure!

BRIDE. Or plenty of bitterness.

SERVANT. I'm going to put the orange-blossom from here to here, so that the wreath will crown your hair. (*She tries on the sprigs of orange-blossom.*)

BRIDE (*she looks at herself in the mirror*). Give it to me. (*She takes the orange-blossom, looks at it and lowers her head dejectedly.*)

SERVANT. What's the matter?

BRIDE. Leave me alone!

SERVANT. It's no time to be feeling sad. (*Spiritedly.*) Give me the orange-blossom. (*The* BRIDE *throws the wreath away.*) Child! Don't tempt fate by throwing the flowers on the floor! Look at me now. Don't you want to get married? Tell me. You can still change your mind. (*She gets up.*)

BRIDE. Dark clouds. A cold wind here inside me. Doesn't everyone feel it?

SERVANT. Do you love your young man?

BRIDE. I love him.

SERVANT. Yes, yes, of course you do.

BRIDE. But it's a very big step.

SERVANT. It has to be taken.

BRIDE. I've already agreed to take it.

SERVANT. I'll fix the wreath for you.

BRIDE (*she sits down*). Hurry, they must be almost here.

SERVANT. They'll have been on the road at least two hours.

BRIDE. How far is it from here to the church?

SERVANT. Five leagues if you go by the stream. If you take the road it's twice as far.

The BRIDE *gets up and the* SERVANT *is excited as she observes her.*

Oh let the bride awaken now
On this her wedding day.
Oh let the rivers of the world
Now bear your bridal-crown away.

BRIDE (*smiling*). Come on.

SERVANT (*she kisses her with feeling and dances around her.*)

Oh let the bride awaken now
To sprig of flowering laurel green.
Oh let the bride awaken now
And by the laurel trees be seen!

A loud knocking is heard.

BRIDE. Open it. It must be the first of the guests. (*She goes out.*)

The SERVANT *opens the door. She is startled.*

SERVANT. You?

LEONARDO. Me. Good morning.

SERVANT. The very first to arrive!

LEONARDO. Haven't I been invited then?

SERVANT. Yes.

LEONARDO. So I'm here.

SERVANT. Where's your wife?

LEONARDO. I came on horseback. She's coming by road.

SERVANT. Did you meet anyone else?

LEONARDO. I rode past them.

SERVANT. You'll kill the animal racing him like that.

LEONARDO. If he dies, he dies!

Pause.

SERVANT. Sit yourself down. There's no one up yet.

LEONARDO. Where's the bride?

SERVANT. I'm going to dress her this very minute.

LEONARDO. She'll be happy I expect! The bride!

SERVANT (*changing the subject*). How's the child?

LEONARDO. Child?

SERVANT. Your little son.

LEONARDO (*recalling, as if in a dream*). Ah!

SERVANT. Is he coming with them?

LEONARDO. No.

Pause. Voices singing in the distance.

VOICES. Let the bride awaken now
    On this her wedding day.

LEONARDO. Let the bride awaken now
    On this her wedding day.

SERVANT. It's the guests. Still a long way off.

LEONARDO (*getting up*). I suppose the bride will be wearing a big wreath of flowers? It shouldn't be so big. Something smaller would suit her better. Did the bridegroom bring the orange-blossom so she can wear it on her heart?

BRIDE (*she appears still in petticoats and with the wreath of flowers in place*). He brought it.

SERVANT (*strongly*). Don't come out like that.

BRIDE. What's the matter? (*Seriously.*) Why do you want to know if they brought the orange-blossom? What are you hinting at?

LEONARDO. What would I be hinting at? (*Moving closer.*) You, you know me, you know I'm not hinting. Tell me. What was I to you? Open up your memory, refresh it. But two oxen and a broken-down shack are almost nothing. That's the thorn.

BRIDE. Why have you come?

LEONARDO. To see your wedding.

BRIDE. I saw yours too!

LEONARDO. You fixed that, you made it with your own two hands. They can kill me, but they can't spit on me. Now silver, shine as it may, can often spit.

BRIDE. That's a lie.

LEONARDO. I don't want to speak out. I'm a man of honour and I don't want all these hills to have to listen to my complaints.

BRIDE. Mine would be louder.

SERVANT. This argument mustn't go on. You mustn't talk about what's gone. (*The* SERVANT *looks anxiously towards the doors.*)

BRIDE. She's right. I shouldn't even be talking to you. But it makes my blood boil that you should come to watch me and spy on my wedding and make insinuations about the orange-blossom. Go and wait for your wife outside.

LEONARDO. Can't we talk, you and me?

SERVANT (*angrily*). No: you can't talk.

LEONARDO. From the day of my wedding I've thought night and day about whose fault it was, and every time I think I find another fault that eats the old one up, but it's always someone's fault!

BRIDE. A man with a horse knows lots of things and can do a lot to take advantage of a girl abandoned in a desert. But I've got my pride. Which is why I'm getting married. And I'll shut myself away with my husband, and I'll love him above everything.

LEONARDO. Pride will get you nowhere! (*He approaches her.*)

BRIDE. Don't come near me!

LEONARDO. To keep quiet and burn is the greatest punishment we can heap upon ourselves. What use was pride to me and not seeing you and leaving you awake night after night? No use! It only brought the fire down on top of me! You think that time heals and walls conceal, and it's not true, not true! When the roots of things go deep, no one can pull them up!

BRIDE (*trembling*). I can't hear you. I can't hear your voice. It's as if I'd drunk a bottle of anise and fallen asleep on a bedspread of roses. And it drags me along, and I know that I'm drowning, but I still go on.

SERVANT (*seizing* LEONARDO *by the lapels*). You should leave now!

LEONARDO. It's the last time I'm going to speak to her. There's nothing to be afraid of.

BRIDE. And I know I'm mad, and I know that my heart's putrified from holding out, and here I am, soothed by the sound of his voice, by the sight of his arms moving.

LEONARDO. I won't be at peace with myself if I don't tell you all this. I got married. You get married now!

SERVANT (*to* LEONARDO). She will!

VOICES (*singing nearer*).
   Oh let the bride awaken now
   On this her wedding day!

BRIDE. Let the bride awaken!

She runs out to her room.

SERVANT. The guests are here. (*To* LEONARDO.) Don't you go near her again.

LEONARDO. Don't worry.

He goes out stage-left. It starts to get light.

FIRST GIRL (*entering*).
   Let the bride awaken now
   On this her wedding day;
   Begin the dance, let flowers now
   Your balconies array.

VOICES. Let the bride awaken!

SERVANT (*whipping up enthusiasm*).
  Let the bride awaken
  To the bright display
  Of love's rich green bouquet.
  May she awaken now
  To trunk and flowering bough
  Of laurel on her wedding day.
SECOND GIRL (*entering*).
  Let her awaken.
  Her long hair covers her throat.
  White as snow is her petticoat.
  Leather and silver on her feet.
  Head adorned by jasmine sweet.
SERVANT. Oh, shepherd-girl,
  The moon appears above.
FIRST GIRL. Oh, handsome lad,
  Leave your hat in the olive grove.
FIRST YOUTH (*enters, holding aloft his hat*).
  Let the bride awaken
  To welcome the wedding-guests.
  Through distant fields they move ahead.
  Trays of dahlias are their gifts,
  Loaves of consecrated bread.
VOICES. May the bride awaken!
SECOND GIRL. The bride
  Puts on her crown of flowers.
  The groom
  Secures it with golden ribbons.
SERVANT. By the grape-fruit tree
  The bride awake shall be.
THIRD GIRL (*entering*).
  By the orange-grove
  Spoon and cloth, his gifts of love.

    Three GUESTS *enter.*

FIRST YOUTH. Sweet dove, awaken!
  The dawn scrubs bright
  The shadowy bells of night.
GUEST. Bride, oh fair white bride,
  Today a maiden she.
  Tomorrow a wife shall be.
FIRST GIRL. Come down, dark girl,
  Trail behind your silken train.
GUEST. Come down, little dark one,
  For morning dew's like icy rain.
FIRST YOUTH. Awaken, bride, awaken.
  Orange-blossom the breeze shall stain.
SERVANT. A tree I shall embroider,
  Adorned with ribbons of darkest red.
  On every one a child, and this:
  'Long life to them when they are wed.'
VOICES. Let the bride awaken!
FIRST YOUTH. On this her wedding day!
GUEST. On this your wedding day
  How handsome you shall be.
  True flower of the mountain,
  Wife of a captain worthy.
FATHER (*entering*). Wife of a true captain,
  The bridegroom takes her with him.
  He comes to claim his treasure,
  Accompanied by oxen.
THIRD GIRL. The bridegroom
  Is a golden flower.
  With every step
  Carnations shower.
SERVANT. Oh, lucky child!
SECOND YOUTH. Let the bride awaken.
SERVANT. Oh, lovely bride!
FIRST GIRL. The wedding
  From every window calls.

SECOND GIRL. Let the bride appear.
FIRST GIRL. Let the bells ring,
  Let the bells shout!
FIRST YOUTH. She comes! The bride is here.
SERVANT. Like a great bull, the wedding
  Begins to stir.

> *The* BRIDE *appears. She wears a black dress in the style of 1900, with a bustle and a long train of pleated gauze and heavy lace. On her hair, which falls across her forehead, she wears a wreath of orange-blossom. The sound of guitars. The* GIRLS *kiss the* BRIDE.

THIRD GIRL. What perfume did you put on your hair?
BRIDE (*laughing*). None.
SECOND GIRL (*looking at her dress*). The material's wonderful!
FIRST YOUTH. Here's the bridegroom!
BRIDEGROOM. Welcome!
FIRST GIRL (*placing a flower behind his ear*).
  The bridegroom
  Is a golden flower.
SECOND GIRL. His eyes communicate
  His joy to ours.

> *The* BRIDEGROOM *goes over to the* BRIDE.

BRIDE. Why did you put those shoes on?
BRIDEGROOM. They look more cheerful than the black ones.
LEONARDO'S WIFE (*entering and kissing the* BRIDE).
  Good health!

> *Everyone chatters excitedly.*

LEONARDO (*entering like someone performing a duty*).
  On your wedding day
  This crown you shall wear.

WIFE. So the fields will be gladdened
  With the dew of your hair.

MOTHER (*to the* FATHER). Are they here too?

FATHER. They are family. Today's a day for forgiveness.

MOTHER. I'll put up with it but I shan't forgive.

BRIDEGROOM. With the crown it's a joy to look at you!

BRIDE. Let's get to the church quickly.

BRIDEGROOM. Why the hurry?

BRIDE. I want to be your wife and be alone with you and
  not hear any other voice but yours.

BRIDEGROOM. That's what I want!

BRIDE. And to see only your eyes. And to have you hold
  me so tight that, even if my mother were to call me, my
  dead mother, I couldn't free myself from you.

BRIDEGROOM. My arms are strong. I'm going to hold
  you for forty years without stopping.

BRIDE (*dramatically, taking his arms*). For ever!

FATHER. Let's go quickly! Bring the horses and the carts!
  The sun has risen.

MOTHER. Drive carefully. Let's hope nothing goes
  wrong.

  The great door opens back-stage. They begin to leave.

SERVANT (*crying*). When you leave your home,
  Oh maiden white,
  Remember you leave,
  A star shining bright.

FIRST GIRL. Clean your body, clean your dress.
  Leaving home, bride to be blessed.

  They continue leaving.

SECOND GIRL. Leaving your home
  For the church's blessing!

SERVANT. The breeze in sand
  bright flowers leaves!

THIRD GIRL. Oh, white young girl!

SERVANT. Dark breeze the lace
  Of her mantilla weaves.

They leave. Guitars, castanets and tambourines are heard.
LEONARDO *and his* WIFE *are left alone.*

WIFE. Let's go.

LEONARDO. Where to?

WIFE. To the church. But you aren't going on horseback.
  You are coming with me.

LEONARDO. In the cart?

WIFE. How else?

LEONARDO. I'm not the kind of man to go by cart.

WIFE. And I'm not the kind of woman to go to a wedding
  without her husband. I can't put up with it any
  more!

LEONARDO. Neither can I!

WIFE. Why are you looking at me like that? A thorn in
  each eye!

LEONARDO. Let's go.

WIFE. I don't know what's happening. But I think and
  I don't want to think. One thing I do know. I've already
  been thrown aside. But I've got a child. And another
  one coming. It's the way things are. My mother's fate was
  the same. But I won't be moved from here. (*Voices off.*)

VOICES. When you leave your home
  For the church's blessing,
  Remember you leave
  Like a bright star shining!

WIFE (*weeping*). Remember you leave,
  A bright star shining
  That's how I left my house too. The whole world
  was mine.

LEONARDO (*getting up*). Let's go.

WIFE. But with me!

LEONARDO. Yes. (*Pause.*) Come on then! (*They go out.*)

VOICES. When you leave your home
   For the church's blessing,
   Remember you leave
   Like a bright star shining.

Slow curtain.

Scene Two

Outside the BRIDE's *cave. Interplay of grey, white, and cold blues. Large prickly pears. Dark and silver tones. Background of plains the colour of biscuit, and everything hard as if it were a landscape in popular ceramic.*

SERVANT (*arranging glasses and trays on a table*).
   Turning,
   The wheel was turning
   And the water was flowing;
   For the wedding-night's coming.
   Let the branches now part,
   And the moon shine bright
   On her balcony white.

   (*Loudly.*) Put out the tablecloths.

   (*In a poetic voice.*) Singing,
   Bride and groom singing,
   And the water was flowing;
   For the wedding-night's coming.
   See the frost's cold brightness.
   Let the almond's bitterness
   Be honey's sweetness.

   (*Loudly.*) Get the wine ready.

(*In a poetic voice.*) Lovely girl,
Oh, loveliest of all.
See the water flowing,
For your wedding-night's coming.
Pull your skirts in tight,
Hide beneath your husband's wing
And never leave him.
For your husband's a dove
Whose breast is burning,
As the fields are waiting
For fresh blood running.
Turning,
The wheel was turning
And the water was flowing.
Your wedding-night's coming
And the water's gleaming.

MOTHER (*entering*). At last!

FATHER. Are we the first?

SERVANT. No. It's a while since Leonardo got here with his wife. They drove like demons. The wife was dead with fright. They made the journey as if they'd come on horseback.

FATHER. That one looks for trouble. He hasn't got good blood.

MOTHER. What blood could he have? The blood of his entire family. It comes from his great-grandfather, who started the killing, and it spreads through the whole breed, all of them knife-handlers and smiling hypocrites.

FATHER. Let's leave it!

SERVANT. How can she leave it?

MOTHER. It hurts to the ends of my veins. On the face of every one of them I can only see the hand that killed what was mine. Do you see me? Do I seem mad to you? Well I am mad from not being able to shout what my heart demands. There's a scream here in my heart that's always rising up, and I have to force it down again and hide it in these shawls. They've taken my dead ones from me and I have to be silent. And because of that people criticize. (*She removes her shawl.*)

FATHER. Today's no day to remember those things.

MOTHER. When I start to talk, I have to speak out. And today even more. Because today I'm left alone in my house.

FATHER. In the hope of having company.

MOTHER. That is my hope: grandchildren. (*They sit.*)

FATHER. I want them to have many. This land needs arms that are not paid for. You have to wage a constant battle with the weeds, with the thistles, with the stones that come up from who knows where. And these arms must belong to the owners, so that they can punish and master, so that they can make the seed flourish. Many sons are needed.

MOTHER. And some daughters! Men are like the wind. In the nature of things they have to handle weapons. Girls never go into the street.

FATHER (*happily*). I think they'll have both.

MOTHER. My son will cover her well. He's of good seed. His father could have had many sons with me.

FATHER. What I'd like is that this should happen in a single day. That straight away they should have two or three boys.

MOTHER. But it's not like that. It takes a long time. That's why it's so terrible to see your blood spilt on the ground. A fountain that spurts for a minute and has cost us years. When I reached my son, he was lying in the middle of the road. I wet my hands with his blood and I licked them with my tongue. Because it was mine. You don't know what that means. I'd put the earth soaked by it in a monstrance of glass and topaz.

FATHER. There's something to hope for now. My

daughter's wide-hipped and your son's strong.

MOTHER. So I'm hoping. (*They rise.*)

FATHER. Get the trays of wheat ready.

SERVANT. They are ready.

LEONARDO'S WIFE (*entering*). Good luck for the future!

MOTHER. Thank you.

LEONARDO. Is there going to be a celebration?

FATHER. A small one. The people can't stay for long.

SERVANT. Here they are!

> The GUESTS *enter in happy groups. The* BRIDAL COUPLE *enter arm in arm.* LEONARDO *leaves.*

BRIDEGROOM. There was never a wedding with so many people.

BRIDE (*darkly*). Never.

FATHER. It was magnificent.

MOTHER. Whole branches of families were there.

BRIDEGROOM. People who never went out of the house.

MOTHER. Your father sowed the seed. Now you reap the harvest.

BRIDEGROOM. There were cousins of mine I didn't even know.

MOTHER. All the people from the coast.

BRIDEGROOM (*happily*). They were scared of the horses. (*They talk.*)

MOTHER (*to the* BRIDE). What are you thinking?

BRIDE. Nothing.

MOTHER. Your blessings weigh heavily. (*Guitars are heard.*)

BRIDE. Like lead.

MOTHER (*strongly*). But they shouldn't. You should be as light as a dove.

BRIDE. Are you staying here tonight?

MOTHER. No. My house is empty.

BRIDE. You ought to stay!

FATHER (*to the* MOTHER). Look at the dance they are forming. Dances from the seashore right over there.

LEONARDO *enters and sits down. His* WIFE *is behind him, standing stiffly.*

MOTHER. They are my husband's cousins. As hard as stones when it comes to dancing.

FATHER. It's a joy to see them. What a change for this house! (*He leaves.*)

BRIDEGROOM (*to the* BRIDE). Did you like the orange-blossom?

BRIDE (*looking at him fixedly*). Yes.

BRIDEGROOM. It's all made of wax. It'll last for ever. I'd like you to have worn them all over your dress.

BRIDE. There's no need for that.

LEONARDO *goes off to the right.*

FIRST GIRL. We'll take your pins out.

BRIDE (*to the* BRIDEGROOM). I'll be back in a minute.

WIFE. I hope you'll be happy with my cousin!

BRIDEGROOM. I'm sure I will.

WIFE. The two of you here; never going out, building a home. I wish I lived as far away as this.

BRIDEGROOM. Why don't you buy land? The mountain's cheap and it's better for bringing up children.

WIFE. We've got no money. And the way we are going!

BRIDEGROOM. Your husband's a good worker.

WIFE. Yes, but he likes to fly around too much. From one thing to another. He's not a steady person.

SERVANT. Aren't you having anything? I'll wrap some wine-cakes for your mother. She really likes them.

BRIDEGROOM. Give her three dozen.

WIFE. No, no. Half a dozen will be quite enough.

BRIDEGROOM. It's a special day.

WIFE (*to the* SERVANT). Where's Leonardo?

SERVANT. I haven't seen him.

BRIDEGROOM. He must be with the guests.

WIFE. I'll go and see. (*She leaves.*)

SERVANT. That's beautiful.

BRIDEGROOM. Aren't you dancing?

SERVANT. There's no one will dance with me.

> *Two* GIRLS *pass across the background; during the entire scene the background will be a lively interplay of figures.*

BRIDEGROOM (*happy*). That's because they don't understand. Lively old women like you dance better than young girls.

SERVANT. Are you trying to flirt with me, boy? What a family you are! Men amongst men! When I was a child I saw your grandfather. What a man! As if a mountain was getting married!

BRIDEGROOM. I'm not as big as that.

SERVANT. But the same twinkle in your eyes. Where's the girl?

BRIDEGROOM. Taking off her head-dress.

SERVANT. Look! For the middle of the night, since you won't be sleeping, I've prepared some ham, and some big glasses of old wine. In the bottom part of the cupboard. Just in case you need it.

BRIDEGROOM. I don't eat in the middle of the night.

SERVANT (*teasing*). If you don't, your wife then. (*She goes out.*)

FIRST YOUTH (*entering*). You've got to have a drink with us.

BRIDEGROOM. I'm waiting for my wife.

SECOND YOUTH. You'll have her in the early hours.

FIRST YOUTH. When it's best!

SECOND YOUTH. Only for a minute!

BRIDEGROOM. Alright.

> *They leave. Sounds of great excitement. The* BRIDE *appears. From the opposite side two* GIRLS *run to meet her.*

FIRST GIRL. Who did you give the first pin to? Me or her?

BRIDE. I don't remember.

FIRST GIRL. You gave it to me here.

SECOND GIRL. You gave it to me, in front of the altar.

BRIDE (*uneasy, with a sense of great inner conflict*). I don't know.

FIRST GIRL. I wish you'd . . .

BRIDE (*interrupting*). And I don't care. I've got lots of things on my mind.

SECOND GIRL. I'm sorry.

LEONARDO *crosses the back-stage.*

BRIDE (*she sees* LEONARDO). And it's a difficult time!

FIRST GIRL. Well, we don't know!

BRIDE. You'll know when your time comes. It's a difficult step to take.

FIRST GIRL. Are you angry?

BRIDE. No. I'm sorry.

SECOND GIRL. What for? But the two pins are for getting married, right?

BRIDE. Both of them.

FIRST GIRL. We'll see which one of us gets married first.

BRIDE. Are you so anxious?

SECOND GIRL (*coyly*). Yes.

BRIDE. But why?

FIRST GIRL. Well . . . (*Embracing the second girl.*)
    They run away. The BRIDEGROOM *enters slowly and embraces the* BRIDE *from behind.*

BRIDE (*very startled*). Don't.

BRIDEGROOM. Are you frightened of me?

BRIDE. Oh! It's you!

BRIDEGROOM. Who else? (*Pause.*) Me or your father.

BRIDE. Yes.

BRIDEGROOM. Though your father would have hugged you more gently.

BRIDE (*gloomily*). Yes.

BRIDEGROOM. Because he's old. (*He embraces her strongly and a bit roughly.*)

BRIDE (*curtly*). Stop it!

BRIDEGROOM. Why? (*He releases her.*)

BRIDE. Well . . . the guests. They can see us.

The SERVANT *crosses back-stage again, without looking at the* BRIDE *and* BRIDEGROOM.

BRIDEGROOM. So? We've taken our vows.

BRIDE. Yes, but leave me be . . . Now.

BRIDEGROOM. What's the matter? It's as if you are frightened.

BRIDE. It's nothing. Don't go.

LEONARDO'*s* WIFE *enters.*

WIFE. I don't mean to interrupt . . .

BRIDE. What is it?

WIFE. Did my husband come through here?

BRIDEGROOM. No.

WIFE. It's just that I can't find him, and the horse isn't in the stable.

BRIDEGROOM (*happily*). He's probably gone for a ride.

The WIFE *goes out, disturbed. The* SERVANT *enters.*

SERVANT. Aren't you pleased with all these good wishes?

BRIDEGROOM. I want it to be over and done with. My wife's a bit tired.

SERVANT. What's the matter, child?

BRIDE. It's as if someone's struck me on the head!

SERVANT. A bride from these mountains has to be strong. (*To the* BRIDEGROOM.) You are the only one who can cure her, since she's yours. (*She runs out.*)

BRIDEGROOM (*embracing her*). Let's go and dance for a bit. (*He kisses her.*)

BRIDE (*disturbed*). No. I want to lie down on the bed.

BRIDEGROOM. I'll come with you.

BRIDE. No! Not with all these people here! What would they say? Let me rest for a moment.

BRIDEGROOM. Whatever you want. But don't be like this tonight!

BRIDE (*at the door*). I'll be better tonight.

BRIDEGROOM. I hope you will.

The MOTHER *enters.*

MOTHER. Son.

BRIDEGROOM. Where've you been?

MOTHER. In the middle of all that noise. Are you happy?

BRIDEGROOM. Yes.

MOTHER. Where's your wife?

BRIDEGROOM. Having a bit of a rest. A bad day for brides!

MOTHER. A bad day? The only good one. For me it was like an inheritance.

The SERVANT *enters and goes towards the* BRIDE'*s room.*

The breaking-up of soil, the planting of new trees!

BRIDEGROOM. Are you thinking of going?

MOTHER. Yes. I must be at home.

BRIDEGROOM. You'll be alone.

MOTHER. No. My head's full of things and of men and fights.

BRIDEGROOM. But fights that aren't fights any more.

The SERVANT *enters quickly; she runs off via the back-stage area.*

MOTHER. As long as you live, you struggle.

BRIDEGROOM. I'll always do what you tell me.

MOTHER. Try to be loving towards your wife, and if you find her uppity or stand-offish, give her a hug that hurts her a bit, a strong embrace, a bite, and then a gentle kiss. Not to annoy her, just to make her feel that you are the man, the master, the one who gives the orders. That's what I learned from your father. And because you don't have him, I must be the one to teach you how to be strong.

BRIDEGROOM. I'll always do what you want me to.

FATHER (*entering*). Where's my daughter?

BRIDEGROOM. She's inside.

FIRST GIRL. Let's have the bride and groom – we are going to do the round dance.

FIRST YOUTH (*to the* BRIDEGROOM). You are going to lead.

FATHER (*entering*). She isn't there.

BRIDEGROOM. No?

FATHER. She must have gone up to the balcony.

BRIDEGROOM. I'll go and see! (*He goes out.*)

A lot of noise and guitars.

FIRST GIRL. They've started! (*She leaves.*)

BRIDEGROOM (*entering*). She's not there.

MOTHER (*uneasily*). No?

FATHER. Where can she be?

SERVANT (*entering*). The girl, where is she?

MOTHER (*sombrely*). We don't know.

The BRIDEGROOM *goes out. Three* GUESTS *enter.*

FATHER (*dramatically*). But isn't she at the dance?

SERVANT. She's not at the dance.

FATHER (*strongly*). There's a crowd of people there. Look!

SERVANT. I've looked already.

FATHER (*darkly*). Well, where is she?

BRIDEGROOM (*entering*). No sign of her. Nowhere.

MOTHER (*to the* FATHER). What is this? Where is your daughter?

LEONARDO's WIFE *enters.*

WIFE. They've run away! They've run away! Her and Leonardo. On horseback! Arms around one another!

Like a flash of lightning!

FATHER. It's not true! Not my daughter!

MOTHER. Yes. Your daughter! A plant from a wicked mother, and him, him too, him! But now she's my son's wife.

BRIDEGROOM (*entering*). We'll go after them! Who's got a horse?

MOTHER. Who's got a horse? Now! Who's got a horse? I'll give him everything I have. My eyes. Even my tongue . . .

VOICE. I'll go!

MOTHER (*to her son*). Go! After them! (*He goes out with two young men.*) No. Don't go! Those people kill quickly and well . . . But yes! Go on! I'll follow.

FATHER. It can't be her. Perhaps she's thrown herself into the water-tank.

MOTHER. Only decent and clean girls throw themselves into the water. Not that one! But now she's my son's wife. Two sides. Now there are two sides here. (*They all enter.*) My family and yours. All of you must go. Shake the dust from your shoes. Let's go and help my son. (*The people split into two groups.*) He's got plenty of family: his cousins from the coast and all those from inland. Go out from here! Search all the roads. The hour of blood has come again. Two sides. You on yours, me on mine. After them! Get after them!

Curtain.

Act III

Scene One

A forest. It is night. Great moist tree trunks. A gloomy atmosphere. Two violins can be heard. Three WOODCUTTERS *appear.*

FIRST WOODCUTTER. Have they found them?

SECOND WOODCUTTER. No. But they are looking for them everywhere.

THIRD WOODCUTTER. They'll find them soon.

SECOND WOODCUTTER. Shhh!

THIRD WOODCUTTER. What?

SECOND WOODCUTTER. They seem to be coming near on all the roads at once.

FIRST WOODCUTTER. When the moon rises they'll see them.

SECOND WOODCUTTER. They should leave them alone.

FIRST WOODCUTTER. The world's big. Everyone can live in it.

THIRD WOODCUTTER. You have to follow your instinct. They were right to run away.

FIRST WOODCUTTER. They were deceiving each other. In the end the blood was strongest.

THIRD WOODCUTTER. The blood!

FIRST WOODCUTTER. You have to follow the blood's path.

SECOND WOODCUTTER. But blood that sees the light, the earth drinks it.

FIRST WOODCUTTER. What of it? Better to be a bloodless

74

corpse than alive and your blood putrid.

THIRD WOODCUTTER. Be quiet.

FIRST WOODCUTTER. Why? Can you hear something?

THIRD WOODCUTTER. I can hear the crickets, the frogs, the night lying in wait.

FIRST WOODCUTTER. But no sound of the horse.

FIRST WOODCUTTER. Now he'll be loving her.

SECOND WOODCUTTER. Her body for him, his body for her.

THIRD WOODCUTTER. They'll find them and they'll kill them.

FIRST WOODCUTTER. But they'll have mixed their blood by then. They'll be like two empty pitchers, like two dry streams.

SECOND WOODCUTTER. There are lots of clouds. Maybe the moon won't come out.

THIRD WOODCUTTER. Moon or no moon, the bridegroom will find them. I saw him leave. Like a raging star. His face the colour of ash. He contained the fate of his family.

FIRST WOODCUTTER. His family of dead men in the middle of the street.

SECOND WOODCUTTER. Yes.

THIRD WOODCUTTER. Do you think they can break through the circle?

SECOND WOODCUTTER. It's hard. There are knives and shotguns for ten leagues around.

THIRD WOODCUTTER. He has a good horse.

SECOND WOODCUTTER. But he's got a woman with him.

FIRST WOODCUTTER. We are close now.

SECOND WOODCUTTER. A tree with forty branches. We'll soon have it cut.

THIRD WOODCUTTER. The moon's coming out now. Let's hurry.

To the left, a patch of light.

FIRST WOODCUTTER. Oh rising moon!
  Moon on the great leaves
SECOND WOODCUTTER. Fill the blood with jasmine!
FIRST WOODCUTTER. Oh lonely moon!
  Moon on the green leaves!
SECOND WOODCUTTER. Silver on the bride's face!
THIRD WOODCUTTER. Oh evil moon!
  Leave for their love a shadowy branch ...
FIRST WOODCUTTER. Oh sad moon!
  Leave for their love a branch in shadow!

> *They leave. In the light stage-left the* MOON *enters. The* MOON *is a young woodcutter with a white face. The stage takes on an intense blue light.*

MOON. Round swan on the river,
  Eye of the cathedrals,
  False dawn amongst the leaves
  Am I; they shall not escape!
  Who is hiding? Who is sobbing
  In the thick brush of the valley?
  The moon places a knife
  Abandoned in the sky,
  That is a leaden ambush
  And longs to be the pain of blood.
  Let me come in! I come frozen
  From walls and windows!
  Open up roofs and hearts
  Where I can warm myself!
  I am cold! My ashes
  Of dreaming metal
  Seek the crest of fire
  Through mountains and through streets.
  But the snow bears me
  On its back of jasper,
  And water drowns me

Cold and hard in pools.
And so tonight there'll be
Red blood to fill my cheeks,
And the rushes forming clusters
At the wide feet of the wind.
Let there be no shadow, no hidden corner
To which they can escape!
For I want to enter a breast
Where I can warm myself!
A heart for me!
Warm!, that will spill
Over the mountains of my breast;
Let me come in, oh, let me in!

(*To the branches.*) I don't want shadows. My rays
Must enter everywhere,
And let there be among dark trunks
A murmur of gleaming light,
So that tonight there'll be
Red blood to fill my cheeks,
And the rushes forming clusters
At the wide feet of the wind.
Who is hiding? Come out, I say!
No! They shan't get away!
For I shall make the horse shine
With fever bright as diamond.

> The MOON *disappears amongst the tree trunks and the stage
> becomes dark. An old* BEGGAR WOMAN *appears completely
> covered in thin dark-green cloth. Her feet are bare. Her face
> can hardly be seen amongst the folds. She is Death.*

BEGGAR WOMAN. The moon goes, and they come near.
  From here they shan't move. The river's murmur
  Shall drown with the whisper of the trees
  The torn flight of their screams.
  It shall be here, and soon. I'm tired.

They're opening the coffins, and white linen
waits, spread on bedroom floors,
For the weight of bodies with torn throats.
No bird shall awaken, and the breeze,
Gathering their cries in her skirt,
Shall fly with them over black tree-tops
Or bury them in soft slime.

(*Impatient.*) That moon! That moon!

The MOON *appears. The intense blue light returns.*

MOON. Now they come near.
Some through the ravine, others by the river.
I shall light up the stones. What do you need?

BEGGAR WOMAN. Nothing.

MOON. The wind is starting to blow hard, and double-
edged.

BEGGAR WOMAN.
Light up the waistcoat, open the buttons,
For then the knives will know their path.

MOON. But let them die slowly. And let the blood
Place between my fingers its soft whistle.
See how my ashen valleys are awakening
With longing for this fountain and its trembling rush.

BEGGAR WOMAN. We mustn't let them get beyond the
stream. Quiet!

MOON. There they come! (*He leaves. The stage is dark.*)

BEGGAR WOMAN.
Quickly! Lots of light! Do you hear me?
They can't escape!

The BRIDEGROOM *and the* FIRST YOUTH *appear. The*
BEGGAR WOMAN *sits and covers her face with her cloak.*

BRIDEGROOM. This way.

FIRST YOUTH. You won't find them.

BRIDEGROOM (*forcefully*). I will find them.

FIRST YOUTH. I think they've gone by some other route.

BRIDEGROOM. No. I heard the sound of galloping a moment ago.

FIRST YOUTH. It must have been another horse.

BRIDEGROOM (*intensely*). Listen. There's only one horse in the whole world, and it's this one. Understand? If you come with me, come with me, but don't talk.

FIRST YOUTH. I wanted to . . .

BRIDEGROOM. Be quiet. I'm certain I'll find them here. You see this arm? Well it's not my arm. It's my brother's arm and my father's and my whole dead family's. And it's got such strength, it could tear this tree from its roots if it wanted to. Let's go quickly. I can feel the teeth of all my loved ones piercing me here so I can't breathe.

BEGGAR WOMAN (*moaning*). Oh!

FIRST YOUTH. Did you hear that?

BRIDEGROOM. Go that way and circle around.

FIRST YOUTH. This is a hunt.

BRIDEGROOM. A hunt. The greatest hunt of all.

The FIRST YOUTH *goes. The* BRIDEGROOM *moves quickly stage-left and stumbles over the* BEGGAR WOMAN.

BEGGAR WOMAN. Oh!

BRIDEGROOM. What do you want?

BEGGAR WOMAN. I'm cold.

BRIDEGROOM. Where are you going?

BEGGAR WOMAN (*always pleading like a beggar*). There . . . it's a long way.

BRIDEGROOM. Where have you come from?

BEGGAR WOMAN. There . . . it's a long way.

BRIDEGROOM. Did you see a man and a woman on horseback, galloping?

BEGGAR WOMAN (*awakening*). Wait . . . (*She looks at him.*) Such a good-looking boy if you were asleep!

BRIDEGROOM. Tell me. Answer. Did you see them?

BEGGAR WOMAN. Wait . . . Such broad shoulders! Why don't you like resting on them instead of walking on feet that are so small?

BRIDEGROOM (*shaking her*). I asked you if you saw them? Have they been this way?

BEGGAR WOMAN (*strongly*). No. They haven't. But they are coming from the hill. Can't you hear them?

BRIDEGROOM. No.

BEGGAR WOMAN. Don't you know the path?

BRIDEGROOM. I'll take it in any case.

BEGGAR WOMAN. I'll come with you. I know this land.

BRIDEGROOM (*impatient*). Let's go. Which way?

BEGGAR WOMAN (*strongly*). That way!

> *They leave quickly. In the distance two violins which represent the forest. The* WOODCUTTERS *return. They carry axes on their shoulders. They move slowly amongst the tree trunks.*

FIRST WOODCUTTER. Oh rising death!
  Death on the great leaves.

SECOND WOODCUTTER. Don't open the gush of blood!

FIRST WOODCUTTER. Oh, lonely death!
  Death on the dry leaves!

THIRD WOODCUTTER. Don't cover the wedding with flowers!

SECOND WOODCUTTER. Oh sad death!
  Leave for their love a green branch.

FIRST WOODCUTTER. Oh terrible death!
  Leave for their love a green branch!

> *They exit as they are speaking.* LEONARDO *and the* BRIDE *appear.*

LEONARDO. Quiet!

BRIDE. I'll go on my own from here.
  You leave me! I want you to turn back.

LEONARDO. I said be quiet!

BRIDE.   With your teeth,
  With your hands, any way you can,
  Tear the metal of this chain
  From my pure throat,
  And leave me locked away
  Here in my house of earth.
  And if you don't want to kill me
  As you'd kill a tiny viper,
  Put the barrel of your gun
  In these bride's hands of mine.
  Oh, what sorrow, what fire
  Sweeps upward through my head!
  What splinters of glass are stuck in my tongue!
LEONARDO. We've taken the step; quiet!
  They are close behind us
  And I'm taking you with me.
BRIDE. It will have to be by force!
LEONARDO. By force? Who was it went
  Down the stairs first?
BRIDE. I did.
LEONARDO.   Who was it put
  A fresh bridle on the horse?
BRIDE. I did. It's true.
LEONARDO.   Which hands
  Strapped the spurs to my boots?
BRIDE. These hands, that are yours,
  That when they see you want
  To break the blue branches
  And the whisper of your veins.
  I love you! I love you! Leave me!
  For if I could kill you,
  I'd place a shroud over you
  Edged with violet.
  Oh, what sorrow, what fire
  Sweeps upward through my head!

LEONARDO.

> What splinters of glass are stuck in my tongue!
> Because I wanted to forget
> And I put a wall of stone
> Between your house and mine.
> It's the truth. Don't you remember?
> And when I saw you from far away
> I threw sand in my eyes.
> But I'd get on the horse
> And the horse would go to your door.
> And then the silver wedding-pins
> Turned my red blood black,
> And our dream began to fill
> My flesh with poisonous weeds.
> Oh, I'm not the one at fault.
> The fault belongs to the earth
> And that scent that comes
> From your breasts and your hair.

BRIDE. Oh, there's no reason! I don't want

> Your blood or your table,
> And there's not a minute of the day
> That I don't want to be with you,
> Because you drag me and I come,
> And you tell me to go back
> And I follow you through the air
> Like a blade of grass.
> I've left a good man
> And all his family
> In the middle of my wedding,
> And wearing my bride's crown.
> The punishment will fall on you,
> And I don't want it to happen.
> Leave me here! You go!
> No one will defend you.

LEONARDO. Birds of early morning
   Are waking in the trees.
   The night is slowly dying
   On the sharp edge of the stone.
   Let's go to a dark corner
   Where I can always love you
   For to me people don't matter,
   Nor the poison they pour on us.

   He embraces her strongly.

BRIDE. And I will sleep at your feet
   And watch over your dreams.
   Naked, looking at the fields,
   (*Powerfully.*) As if I were a bitch.
   Because that's what I am! Oh, I look at you
   And your beauty burns me.
LEONARDO. Flame is fired by flame.
   And the same small flame
   Can kill two ears of grain together.
   Come on!

   He pulls her.

BRIDE. Where are you taking me?
LEONARDO. To a place where they can't go,
   These men who are all around us.
   Where I can look at you!
BRIDE (*sarcastically*). Take me from fair to fair,
   An insult to decent women,
   So that people can see me
   With my wedding sheets displayed
   On the breeze, like banners.
LEONARDO. I want to leave you too,
   If I thought as I ought to think.
   But I go where you go.
   And you too. Take a step. See.

Nails of moonlight join us,
My waist and your hips.

The whole scene is very strong, full of a great sensuality.

BRIDE. Listen!
LEONARDO.   Someone's coming.
BRIDE.   Go quickly!
  It's right that I should die here,
  My feet deep in the water
  And thorns stuck in my head.
  And let the leaves weep for me,
  A woman lost and virgin.
LEONARDO. Be quiet! They are coming up.
BRIDE.   Go!
LEONARDO. Quiet! Don't let them hear us.
  You go first! Come on! Listen!

  The BRIDE *hesitates.*

BRIDE. Both of us!
LEONARDO (*embracing her*). Whatever you want!
  If they separate us, it will be
  Because I am dead.
BRIDE.   I will be dead too.

  They leave embracing each other.

The MOON *appears slowly. The stage takes on a strong blue
light. The two violins are heard. Suddenly two long, piercing
screams and the music of the violins stops. With the second
scream the* BEGGAR WOMAN *appears and stands with
her back to the audience. She opens her cloak and stands centre-
stage like a great bird with huge wings. The* MOON *stops.
The curtain comes down in total silence.*

Scene Two

*A white room with arches and thick walls. To the right and left
white stairs. At the back a great arch and a wall of the same colour.
The floor must also be a dazzling white. This simple room should
have the monumental quality of a church. There must not be any
grey, or shadow, anything that creates perspective.*

Two GIRLS *dressed in dark blue are winding a skein of red wool.*

FIRST GIRL. Oh, wool, oh wool,
   What will you make?
SECOND GIRL. A dress soft as jasmine,
   Cloth paper-thin.
   Begin it at four.
   At ten finishing.
   A thread of my wool's
   A chain for your feet.
   A knot that chokes,
   The bride's bitter wreath.
LITTLE GIRL (*singing*). Did you see the wedding?
FIRST GIRL. No.
LITTLE GIRL   I couldn't go!
   What can have happened
   Where the vine-shoots grow?
   What can have happened
   In the olive grove now?
   What has happened?
   No one's come home
   Did you see the wedding?
SECOND GIRL. We've told you: no.
LITTLE GIRL (*leaving*). And I couldn't go!
SECOND GIRL. Oh wool, oh wool,
   Of what will you sing?
FIRST GIRL. Of wounds like wax,
   And myrtle's ache.
   Of day's long sleep
   And nights awake.

LITTLE GIRL (*at the door*).
  The wool's caught
  On a stone like a knife.
  The blue mountains
  Give it new life.
  It runs, runs, runs,
  By destiny led,
  To cut with a knife
  And take away bread.

  She leaves.

SECOND GIRL. Oh wool, oh wool,
  What will you say?
FIRST GIRL. The lover's dumb,
  The young man red.
  On the silent shore
  I saw them spread.

  She stops and gazes at the wool.

LITTLE GIRL (*appearing at the door*). Run, run, run.
  Bring the wool here.
  Covered in mud
  I feel them come near.
  Their bodies stiff
  And the sheets marble-clear.

  She leaves. Leonardo's WIFE *and* MOTHER-IN-LAW *appear.*

FIRST GIRL. Are they coming?
MOTHER-IN-LAW (*harshly*). We don't know.
SECOND GIRL. What can you tell us about the wedding?
FIRST GIRL. Tell me.
MOTHER-IN-LAW (*curtly*). Nothing.
WIFE. I want to go back to know all of it.
MOTHER-IN-LAW (*strongly*). You, to your house.
  Brave and alone in your house.
  To grow old and weep.

But the door always shut.
Never a soul. Dead or alive.
We'll nail up the windows.
And let the rains and the nights
Fall on the bitter weeds.

WIFE. What could have happened?

MOTHER-IN-LAW.   It doesn't matter.
Cover your face with a veil.
Your children are your children,
There is nothing else. Over your bed
Place a cross of ash
Where once his pillow was.

They leave.

BEGGAR WOMAN (*at the door*). A piece of bread, little
girls.

LITTLE GIRL.   Go away!

The GIRLS *huddle together.*

BEGGAR WOMAN. Why?

LITTLE GIRL. Because you whine. Go away!

FIRST GIRL.   Child!

BEGGAR WOMAN.
I could have asked for your eyes. A cloud
Of birds is following me. Would you like one?

LITTLE GIRL. I want to go home!

SECOND GIRL (*to the* BEGGAR WOMAN). Pay no
attention!

FIRST GIRL. Did you come by the path along the stream?

BEGGAR WOMAN. I did.

FIRST GIRL (*timidly*). Can I ask you something?

BEGGAR WOMAN.
I saw them; they'll be here soon: two rushing streams
Still at last amongst the great stones,
Two men at the horse's feet,

Dead in the beauty of the night.
(*With pleasure.*)Dead, yes, dead!

FIRST GIRL. Be quiet, old woman, be quiet!

BEGGAR WOMAN.

Their eyes broken flowers, and their teeth
Two fistfuls of frozen snow.
Both of them fell, and the bride comes back,
Her skirt and her hair stained with their blood,
Covered by blankets both of them come,
Borne on the shoulders of tall young men.
That's how it was; no more, no less. Fitting.
Over the golden flower, dirty sand.

> *She goes. The* GIRLS *incline their heads and begin to leave rhythmically.*

FIRST GIRL. Dirty sand.

SECOND GIRL.   Over the golden flower.

LITTLE GIRL. Over the golden flower.

They are bringing the dead from the stream.
Dark-skinned the one,
Dark-skinned the other.
Oh, a nightingale's shadow flies and weeps
Over the golden flower!

> *She leaves. The stage is empty. The* MOTHER *appears with a* NEIGHBOUR. *The* NEIGHBOUR *is weeping.*

MOTHER. Be quiet.

NEIGHBOUR. I can't.

MOTHER. I said be quiet. (*At the door.*) Is anyone there? (*She puts her hands to her forehead.*) My son should have answered. But my son's an armful of withered flowers now. My son's a fading voice beyond the mountains. (*Angrily, to the* NEIGHBOUR.) Won't you be quiet? I don't want weeping in this house. Your tears are tears that come from your eyes, that's all. But mine will come, when I'm all alone, from the soles of my feet, from my roots, and they'll burn hotter than blood.

NEIGHBOUR. Come to my house. Don't stay here.

MOTHER. Here. Here's where I want to be. At peace. All of them are dead now. At midnight I'll sleep, I'll sleep and not be afraid of a gun or a knife. Other mothers will go to their windows, lashed by the rain, to see the face of their sons. Not me. From my dream I'll fashion a dove of cold marble that will bear camellias of frost to the graveyard. But no, it's not a graveyard, not a graveyard: a bed of earth, a bed that shelters them and rocks them to sleep in the sky.

A WOMAN *enters, dressed in black. She goes to the right and kneels.*

(*To the* NEIGHBOUR.) Take your hands from your face. We have to face terrible days. I want to see no one. The earth and me. My grief and me. And these four walls. Oh! Oh!

She sits, overcome.

NEIGHBOUR. Have pity on yourself.

MOTHER (*smoothing her hair back*). I have to be calm. (*She sits.*) Because the neighbours will come and I don't want them to see me so poor. So poor! A woman without a single son she can hold to her lips.

The BRIDE *enters. She comes without the orange-blossom and wearing a black shawl.*

NEIGHBOUR (*angrily, seeing the* BRIDE). Where are you going?

BRIDE. I'm coming here.

MOTHER (*to the* NEIGHBOUR). Who is it?

NEIGHBOUR. Don't you know her?

MOTHER. That's why I'm asking who she is. Because I mustn't know her, so I shan't sink my teeth into her neck. Serpent!

She moves towards the BRIDE *threateningly; she stops.*

(*To the* NEIGHBOUR.) You see her? There, weeping, and me calm, without tearing her eyes out. I don't understand myself. Is it because I didn't love my son? But what about his name? Where is his name?

She strikes the BRIDE *who falls to the ground.*

NEIGHBOUR. In the name of God! (*She tries to separate them.*)

BRIDE (*to the* NEIGHBOUR). Leave her. I came so that she could kill me, so that they could bear me away with them. (*To the* MOTHER.) But not with their hands; with iron hooks, with a sickle, and with a force that will break it on my bones. Leave her! I want her to know that I'm clean, that even though I'm mad they can bury me and not a single man will have looked at himself in the whiteness of my breasts.

MOTHER. Be quiet, be quiet! What does that matter to me?

BRIDE. Because I went off with the other one! I went! (*In anguish.*) You would have gone too. I was a woman burning, full of pain inside and out, and your son was a tiny drop of water that I hoped would give me children, land, health; but the other one was a dark river, full of branches, that brought to me the sound of its reeds and its soft song. And I was going with your son, who was like a child of cold water, and the other one sent hundreds of birds that blocked my path and left frost on the wounds of this poor, withered woman, this girl caressed by fire. I didn't want to, listen to me! I didn't want to! Your son was my ambition and I haven't deceived him, but the other one's arm dragged me like a wave from the sea, like the butt of a mule, and would always have dragged me, always, always, even if I'd been an old woman and all the sons of your son had tried to hold me down by my hair !

A NEIGHBOUR *enters.*

MOTHER. She's not to blame! Nor me! (*Sarcastically.*) So
who's to blame? A weak, delicate, restless woman who
throws away a crown of orange-blossom to look for a
piece of bed warmed by another woman!

BRIDE. Be quiet, be quiet! Take your revenge on me!
Here I am! See how soft my throat is; less effort for you
than cutting a dahlia in your garden. But no, not that!
I'm pure, as pure as a new-born child. And strong
enough to prove it to you. Light the fire. We'll put our
hands in it: you for your son; me for my body. You'll be
the first to take them out.

Another NEIGHBOUR *enters.*

MOTHER. What does your honour matter to me? What
does your death matter to me? What does anything
matter to me? Blessed be the wheat, for my sons lie
beneath it. Blessed be the rain, for it washes the faces of
the dead. Blessed be God, for He lays us side by side so
we can rest.

Another NEIGHBOUR *enters.*

BRIDE. Let me weep with you.

MOTHER. Weep. But by the door.

> *The* LITTLE GIRL *enters. The* BRIDE *remains by the door.*
> *The* MOTHER, *centre-stage.*

WIFE (*entering, moving stage-left*).
He was a handsome horseman,
Now a frozen heap of snow.
He rode to fairs and mountains
And the arms of women.
Now the dark moss of night
Forms a crown upon his brow.

MOTHER. Sunflower for your mother,
Mirror of the earth.

Let them place on your breast
A cross of bitter oleander;
A sheet to cover you
Of shining silk,
And let the water form its weeping
Between your still hands.

WIFE. Oh, four young men
Come with tired shoulders!

BRIDE. Oh, four handsome boys
Bear death on high.

MOTHER. Neighbours.

LITTLE GIRL (*at the door*). They are bringing them now.

MOTHER. It's the same.
The cross, the cross.

WOMEN. Sweet nails,
Sweet cross,
Sweet name
of Jesus.

BRIDE. Let the cross protect the living and the dead.

MOTHER. Neighbours: with a knife,
With a small knife,
On a day appointed, between two and three,
The two men killed each other for love.
With a knife,
With a small knife
That barely fits the hand,
But that slides in clean
Through startled flesh
And stops at the place
Where trembles, enmeshed,
The dark root of a scream.

BRIDE. And this is a knife,
A small knife
That barely fits the hand;
Fish without scales or river,

So that on a day appointed, between two and three,
With this knife
Two men are left stiff
And lips turned yellow.
MOTHER. That barely fits the hand,
But that slides in clean
Through startled flesh
And stops there, at the place
Where trembles enmeshed
The dark root of a scream.

The neighbours are kneeling and weeping.

Curtain.

Note on the translation
of *Blood Wedding*

The aim of this translation is to render as accurately as possible both the meaning of Lorca's words and the 'feeling' of the play as a whole. As far as the former is concerned, it is important not to dilute the Spanishness of Lorca's language by seeking approximations or equivalents which will make the dialogue more polished, more acceptable, and ultimately more cosy for an English-speaking audience. The dialogue of *Blood Wedding* is often extremely stark and concise, the exchanges between characters conducted in short, sharp phrases which instantly communicate strong feeling; while intense emotion is expressed in longer, more arching sentences appropriate to the feeling which underlies them. In either case it is essential that an English translation should seek to capture the rhythms of this most 'operatic' and passionate of twentieth-century Spanish dramatists, be it in relation to the prose or the poetry of the play.

The poetry of *Blood Wedding* takes the form of songs in Acts One and Two, while in Act Three the dialogue itself is often in verse. In either case the original is not normally characterized by rhyme but by assonance: the last word of alternate lines has the same two vowels, one stressed, the other unstressed: 'mojádǎ' 'plátǎ', 'relinchá̌bǎ'. Since English cannot easily achieve this effect, I have opted for rhyming patterns in the case of the songs and free verse for the poetry of Act Three.

Despite my intention to translate Lorca with accuracy, it should be understood that this is not a literal translation, which would make it unplayable. My whole purpose is to produce a translation suited to stage performance.

Gwynne Edwards, 1987

Doña Rosita the Spinster

or

The Language of the Flowers

A poem of 1900 Granada,
divided into various gardens,
with scenes of song and dance

Translated by Gwynne Edwards

This translation of *Doña Rosita the Spinster* was first performed at the Theatre Royal, Bristol on 12 October, 1989, with the following cast:

DOÑA ROSITA	Susan Curnow
THE HOUSEKEEPER	Sandra Voe
THE AUNT	Eve Pearce
THE UNCLE	Michael Turner
FIRST SPINSTER/MANOLA	Michelle Butt
SECOND SPINSTER	Petronilla Whitfield
THIRD SPINSTER/MANOLA	Lucinda Smith
THE MOTHER OF THE SPINSTERS	Laura Cox
FIRST MISS AYOLA	Samantha Shaw
SECOND MISS AYOLA/MANOLA	Jane Annesley
THE NEPHEW	Chris Eccleston
THE YOUTH/THE TEACHER OF POLITICAL ECONOMY	Adrian Scarborough
DON MARTIN	Peter Russell

Directed by Phyllida Lloyd
Designed by Anthony Ward
Music Gary Yershon
Movement Petronilla Whitfield
Lighting by Tim Mitchell
Sound by Christopher Johns

Act One

A room leading to a greenhouse.

UNCLE. Where are my seeds?

HOUSEKEEPER. They were here.

UNCLE. Well, they aren't here now.

AUNT. Hellebore, fuchsias and chrysanthemums, violet Louis Passy and silver-white altar with heliotrope points.

UNCLE. It's essential to take care with flowers.

HOUSEKEEPER. If you mean that I . . .

AUNT. Be quiet! Don't answer back!

UNCLE. I mean everyone. Yesterday I found the dahlia seeds trampled into the ground. (*He goes into the greenhouse.*) You don't understand what my greenhouse means. In 1807 the Countess of Wandes produced the musk rose. Since then no one in Granada has managed it except me! Not even the botanist at the university! So you should have more respect for my plants.

HOUSEKEEPER. But don't I respect them?

AUNT. Shhh! You are worse than anyone.

HOUSEKEEPER. Yes, madam. But *I* don't say that with all this spraying and all this water everywhere we'll soon have toads coming out of the sofa!

AUNT. You *do* love sniffing at the flowers!

HOUSEKEEPER. I don't, madam. For me flowers have the smell of a dead child, or a nun, or the altar in a church. Sad things. Where there's an orange or a fine quince, you can keep all your roses! But here . . . roses to the

99

right, basil to the left, anemones, sage, petunias and those new-fangled, fashionable chrysanthemums with heads as scruffy as gypsy girls! Oh, how I'd love to see a pear tree planted in this garden, or a cherry tree or a persimmon!

AUNT. Only so you could eat the fruit!

HOUSEKEEPER. As someone with a mouth . . . They used to say in my village:
The mouth's purpose is to eat,
The legs' purpose is to dance,
And there's a woman's thing . . .

She pauses, goes over to the AUNT *and whispers in her ear.*

AUNT (*crossing herself*). Good Lord!

HOUSEKEEPER (*crossing herself*). Such are the crudities of village life!

ROSITA *rushes in. She wears a rose-coloured dress, in the style of 1900, with leg-of-mutton sleeves and trimmed with braid.*

ROSITA. My hat? Where is my hat? The bells of San Luis have rung thirty times already!

HOUSEKEEPER. I left it on the table.

ROSITA. Well, it's not there.

They hunt for the hat. The HOUSEKEEPER *goes out.*

AUNT. Have you looked in the wardrobe?

The AUNT *goes out.*

HOUSEKEEPER (*entering*). I can't find it.

ROSITA. Can it possibly be that no one knows where my hat is?

HOUSEKEEPER. Wear the blue one with the daisies.

ROSITA. You must be mad.

HOUSEKEEPER. You are even madder.

AUNT (*reappearing*). Come on, here it is!

ROSITA *grabs the hat and rushes out.*

HOUSEKEEPER. She wants everything at top speed. It's today and she already wants it to be the day after tomorrow. She flies off and ... she's slipped through our fingers. When she was small, I had to tell her every day the story about when she'd be an old woman: 'My Rosita's eighty years old now' ... Always the same thing. When have you ever seen her sitting down to do some lace-work or festoon points or close-work on a cap?

AUNT. Never.

HOUSEKEEPER. Always from shout to sheet and sheet to shout, from shout to sheet and sheet to shout!

AUNT. You take care you don't say something you don't intend!

HOUSEKEEPER. If I do, madam, I won't use a word you aren't familiar with already.

AUNT. Of course, I've never liked to say no to her. Who wants to upset a child who has no mother or father?

HOUSEKEEPER. No mother, no father, no puppy to bark for her. But an aunt and an uncle who are a real treasure! (*She embraces the* AUNT.)

UNCLE (*off*). This is really too much!

AUNT. Holy Mother!

UNCLE. They can trample on the seeds if they like, but to pull the leaves off my favourite rose bush – that is insufferable! It means more to me than the musk, hispid, pompon, damask or Queen Elizabeth eglantine. (*To the* AUNT.) Come! Come! See for yourself!

AUNT. Is it ruined?

UNCLE. No, it's not too serious. But it could have been!

HOUSEKEEPER. We'll never hear the end of this!

UNCLE. The question is: who knocked the pot over?

HOUSEKEEPER. Don't look at me!

UNCLE. Was it *me*?

HOUSEKEEPER. And what about cats? What about dogs? What about a gust of wind coming through the window?

AUNT. Come along, now! Sweep out the greenhouse!

HOUSEKEEPER. I can see that no one's allowed to speak in this house!

UNCLE (*enters*). It's a rose you've never seen; a surprise I've prepared for you. The 'rosa declinata' is an incredible flower – with its drooping buds and its thornless inermis. Now isn't that a wonder? Not a single thorn! And then there's the myrtifolia, Belgian in origin, and the sulfurata that glows in the dark. But this one beats them all for being out of the ordinary. Botanists call it the 'Rosa Mutabile', which means 'mutable', that it changes ... This book has an account of it, and a picture. Look! (*He opens the book.*) It's red in the morning. In the evening it turns white. At night the petals fall.

She opens in the morning,
Her colour the deepest red.
Afraid of being burnt by her,
The dew has quickly fled.

At noon her petals, open wide,
Have all the firmness of coral.
The sun looks down to gaze upon
The splendour of its rival.

When birds take to the branches
To announce the approach of sleep,
And evening begins to slip
Into the sea's azure deep.

Then her red grows deadly pale,
Like a cheek by sorrow torn,
And night, approaching softly,
Blows on a metal horn.

The stars advance across the sky,
The wind no longer calls,
As on the edge of darkness,
Her petals begin to fall.

AUNT. Does it have a bud yet?
UNCLE. One, that's opening out.
AUNT. And it lasts just one day?
UNCLE. Only one. I intend to spend that day right next to
it to observe it turning white.
ROSITA (*rushing in*). My parasol!
UNCLE. Her parasol.
AUNT (*shouting*). The parasol!
HOUSEKEEPER (*appearing*). Here's the parasol!

> ROSITA *takes the parasol and kisses her* AUNT *and*
> UNCLE.

ROSITA. How do I look?
UNCLE. Exquisite!
AUNT. No one prettier!
ROSITA (*opening the parasol*). And now?
HOUSEKEEPER. For God's sake close the parasol! It
shouldn't be opened in the house. It brings bad
luck.

By Saint Bartholomew's wheel,
Saint Joseph's magic wand,
And the laurel's blessed flower,
Bad luck's hereby banned
To Jerusalem's far-off land.

> *They all laugh. The* UNCLE *leaves.*

ROSITA (*closing the parasol*). There!
HOUSEKEEPER. Never do that again! Chri . . . stmas!
ROSITA. Goodness me!
AUNT. What were you about to say?
HOUSEKEEPER. But I didn't say it!

ROSITA (*goes out laughing*). See you later!

AUNT. Who's going with you?

ROSITA (*looking in*). I'm going with the girls.

HOUSEKEEPER. And your young man.

AUNT. I think her young man's otherwise engaged.

HOUSEKEEPER. I don't know which I prefer: her fiancé or her.

The AUNT *sits to do lace-work with bobbins.*

A pair of cousins to put on a shelf with the sugar! And if they dropped down dead – God forbid! – we'd need to preserve them and keep them in an alcove with the glassware. Which do you like best? (*She begins to clean.*)

AUNT. I love both of them, as niece and nephew.

HOUSEKEEPER. One for the upper sheet and one for the lower, but . . .

AUNT. Rosita's grown up with me . . .

HOUSEKEEPER. Exactly. I don't believe in blood ties. For me the important thing is this. Blood runs through our veins, but it can't be seen. If we see a second cousin every day, we love him more than a brother who's far away. Why? I'll tell you.

AUNT. Woman, get on with your cleaning.

HOUSEKEEPER. Alright. No one's allowed to open her mouth here. Bring up a pretty little girl for this! Leave your own children in a hut, shivering from hunger!

AUNT. You mean cold.

HOUSEKEEPER. Shivering from everything, so that they can say 'Shut up!' And because I'm a servant I can do nothing but shut up, which is what I do, and I can't answer back and tell you . . .

AUNT. And tell me what?

HOUSEKEEPER. To stop those bobbins clickety-clacking! My head's going to burst with clickety-clacking!

AUNT (*laughing*). Go and see who's just arrived.

The stage is silent except for the clicking of the bobbins.

PEDLAR'S VOICE. Ca-a-amo- o-mile, fine ca-a-amomile from the mountains!

AUNT (*talking aloud to herself*). I need to buy more camomile. Sometimes it's very useful ... When he comes next ... thirty-seven, thirty-eight.

PEDLAR'S VOICE (*far off*). Ca-a-amo-mile from the mountains!

AUNT (*placing a pin*). And forty!

NEPHEW (*entering*). Aunt ...

AUNT (*without looking at him*). Ah, sit down if you like. Rosita's gone out already.

NEPHEW. Who with?

AUNT. With some girl friends. (*Pause. She looks at the* NEPHEW.) Something's wrong.

NEPHEW. Yes.

AUNT (*uneasy*). I can guess what it is. I hope I'm wrong.

NEPHEW. Read this.

AUNT (*reads*). Well, it's to be expected. That's why I was against your engagement to Rosita. I knew that sooner or later you'd have to join your parents. And it's so near, isn't it? Only forty days to get from here to Tucumán! If I were a man, and younger, I'd slap your face ...

NEPHEW. I'm not to blame for loving my cousin. Do you think I want to go? I want to stay here. That's why I've come.

AUNT. Stay! Stay! Your duty is to go. The farm's big and your father's old. It's my responsibility to see that you get on the boat. But you leave me to a life of bitterness. I don't wish to think about your cousin. You are going to pierce her heart with an arrow of purple ribbons. Now she's about to learn that a piece of linen's not just to embroider flowers. It's also to dry one's tears.

NEPHEW. What's your advice?

AUNT. Go. Remember your father is my brother. Here you are ... just passing the time, someone strolling through the pretty little gardens. Over there you'll be a farmer.

NEPHEW. The thing is, I'd like to ...

AUNT. Get married? Are you mad? When you've sorted out your future. As for taking Rosita with you, never! Over my dead body and your uncle's.

NEPHEW. I just thought ... I know very well that I can't. But I want Rosita to wait for me. I'll be back soon.

AUNT. If you don't meet some Tucumán girl first! My tongue should have stuck to the roof of my mouth before I agreed to your engagement. Because my child's left alone between these four walls, and you go free across the sea, up rivers, through grapefruit groves. My child here, one day exactly like the next, and you over there with your horse and your gun for shooting pheasants!

NEPHEW. You've no cause to talk to me like that. I gave my word and I'll keep it. To keep his word my father went to South America, and you know ...

AUNT (*gently*). Not so loud!

NEPHEW. Alright, but don't confuse respect with a lack of conscience.

AUNT (*with irony*). Oh, do forgive me! I'd completely forgotten that you're a man now.

HOUSEKEEPER (*enters weeping*). If he were a man, he wouldn't go!

AUNT (*sternly*). Be quiet!

The HOUSEKEEPER *weeps loudly.*

NEPHEW. I'll be back in a minute. You'd better tell her.

AUNT. Don't worry. Old people are the ones who have to put up with the hard times.

The NEPHEW *leaves.*

HOUSEKEEPER. Oh, God take pity on my child! Take pity! Oh, take pity! These are today's men. I'd stick by the side of this treasure even if I had to beg in the streets. Tears are coming to this house again. Oh, madam! (*Pulling herself together.*) I hope the sea serpent eats him up!

AUNT. God will decide!

HOUSEKEEPER. By the sesame seed,
By the three holy questions
And the cinnamon flower,
Let him have sleepless nights,
Let the seed that he sows die,
And by St Nicholas' well
Let his salt turn to poison.

She takes a jar of water and makes a cross on the ground.

AUNT. Don't put a curse on him. Get on with your work.

The HOUSEKEEPER *leaves. Laughter is heard. The* AUNT *leaves.*

FIRST MANOLA (*entering and closing her parasol*). Oh!

SECOND MANOLA (*as above*). Oh! How cool!

THIRD MANOLA (*as above*). Oh!

ROSITA (*entering and closing her parasol*).
For whom are the sighs
Of my three pretty friends?

MANOLA 1. For no one.

MANOLA 2.　　　For the wind.

MANOLA 3. For a handsome boy who courts me.

ROSITA. Whose hands will pick
The sighs from your lips?

MANOLA 1. A wall.

MANOLA 2.　　　A picture.

MANOLA 3. The lace of my pillow.

ROSITA. I too wish to sigh,
  Oh, my dear, sincere friends!
MANOLA 1. Who gathers your sighs?
ROSITA.   Two eyes
  That make the darkness bright,
  Whose lashes are vines
  Where daylight sleeps.
  Two eyes that, though as black as jet,
  Light, like poppies, the deepest night.
MANOLA 1. Tie your sighs with bright ribbon.
MANOLA 2. Oh!
MANOLA 3.   Happy girl!
MANOLA 1.   Oh, happy one!
ROSITA. Tell me no lies, my friends,
  For I've heard certain tales of you.
MANOLA 1. Tales that are seeds on the wind.
MANOLA 2. Or the whisper of the waves.
ROSITA. Shall I tell you?
MANOLA 1.   Oh, do!
MANOLA 2. Tales like garlands of brightest hue.
ROSITA. Granada, Elvira Street,
  There live the girls who tease,
  Those who visit the Alhambra,
  Alone in twos or threes.

  The first of them is dressed in green,
  The second mauve; the third's encased
  In a Scottish bodice
  With ribbons at her waist.

  The two in front are herons,
  The girl behind a dove.
  Along the avenues of poplar trees
  Mysterious muslins move.

  Oh, how dark the Alhambra is!
  Where do the three girls go?

While the rose and the leaping fountain
Suffer in deepest shadow?

What handsome men await them?
Beneath which myrtle will they rest?
Whose hands will steal the perfume
From the flowers of their breasts?

No one walks with them, no one.
Two herons and a dove.
Behind the leaves are hidden
Men who could give them love.

The cathedral lies in darkness,
Where the breeze softly sings.
The Genil lulls its oxen,
The Dauro the butterflies' wings.

Night approaches slowly,
Shadows upon its face.
A girl displays a pretty shoe
Through petticoats of lace.

The eyes of the eldest are open wide,
The youngest's half-closed in dream.
High-breasted girls, their dresses long,
Who are they, what does it mean?
Handkerchiefs flutter in the wind,
Where, so late, have they been?

Granada, Elvira Street,
There live the girls who tease,
Those who visit the Alhambra,
Alone in twos or threes.

MANOLA 1. Let your tale send out
    Its ripples across Granada's roof.
MANOLA 2. Which of us has a lover?
ROSITA.   None.
MANOLA 2. What is it I tell?

ROSITA   The truth.

MANOLA 3. Our bridal petticoats are edged
With lace of frost.

ROSITA. But ...

MANOLA 1.   The night is our companion.

ROSITA. But ...

MANOLA 2.   And streets in shadow lost.

MANOLA 2. We walk to the Alhambra
Alone in threes and fours.

MANOLA 3. Oh!

MANOLA 2.   Hush!

MANOLA 3.   But why?

MANOLA 1. Let no one know our troubles!

ROSITA. The Alhambra, garden of jasmine and anguish,
Where the moon sleeps.

HOUSEKEEPER (*very sadly*). Child, your aunt's calling you.

ROSITA. Have you been crying?

HOUSEKEEPER (*controlling herself*). No ... it's just that ...
there's something that ...

ROSITA. I'm frightened. What's wrong?

She leaves quickly, looking at the HOUSEKEEPER. *When*
ROSITA *has left, the* HOUSEKEEPER *begins to weep*
silently.

MANOLA 1 (*loudly*). What is it?

MANOLA 2. Tell us!

HOUSEKEEPER. Be quiet!

MANOLA 3 (*quietly*). Bad news?

The HOUSEKEEPER *takes them to the door through which*
ROSITA *left.*

HOUSEKEEPER. She's telling her now.

Pause. They all listen.

MANOLA 1. Rosita's crying. Let's go to her.

HOUSEKEEPER. Come with me. I'll tell you what's

happened. Leave her for now. You can go out by the side gate.

They leave. The stage is empty. A very distant piano plays a Czerny étude. Pause. The NEPHEW *enters and stops in the centre of the room when* ROSITA *also enters. The two stand face to face, looking at each other. The* NEPHEW *moves towards her. She leans her head on his shoulder.*

ROSITA. When your eyes met mine, cousin,
  They did so treacherously.
  When your hands gave me flowers, cousin,
  They did so deceitfully.
  And now, still young, you are leaving me
  To the nightingale's sad song.
  You, whom I loved so truly,
  Can only do me this wrong.
  How can you leave me so cruelly,
  Like the strings of a lute struck dumb?
NEPHEW (*taking her to the 'vis-à-vis' where they sit down*).
  To me your love's precious, cousin,
  More precious than any gold.
  As the nightingale's silent in winter,
  You must resist imagined cold.
  There's no coldness in my going,
  Though my journey's across the sea,
  And the sea offers consolation,
  A quiet tranquillity
  That offers me salvation,
  Should passion seek to destroy me.
ROSITA. One night on my jasmine balcony
  I lay asleep and dreaming,
  And dreamt I saw two cherubs attend
  A rose sick with yearning.
  Her colour was the palest white,
  But she turned the deepest red.

By nature fragile and tender,
Her burning petals bled,
Till, wounded by love's assault,
The rose lay cold and dead.
So I, innocent cousin,
In the garden of myrtle walking,
To the fountain offered my paleness,
To the soft wind my longing.
Like a tender, foolish gazelle,
I dared to look on you lovingly,
At once my heart was pierced
By needles of quivering agony.
Its wounds as red as wallflower
Began to bleed fatally.

NEPHEW. Cousin, I shall come back to you,
I give you my word truly,
In a boat fashioned of gold,
Its sails guided by loyalty.
In sun and shadow, night and day,
I shall dream of you faithfully.

ROSITA. When the spirit's left alone,
Love drips its poison slowly.
With earth and salt it shall weave
The shroud that will soon clothe me.

NEPHEW. When my horse stops to graze
On the grass wet with dew,
When the mist lies on the river,
And the wall of the wind's white through,
When the burning heat of summer
Scorches the blood-red plain,
And the frost's starry needles
Are a bright stab of pain.
Then I will make my promise
And never leave you again.

ROSITA. My dream is to see you come, cousin,
  At night through Granada to me,
  When the light's full of salt, cousin,
  From longing for the sea.
  A lemon grove of yellow,
  Jasmine that's white and bloodless,
  Stones that kill with their hardness,
  All will stop your progress,
  And nards spinning like whirlpools
  Will fill my house with madness.
  Will you ever come back?
NEPHEW.   I promise.
ROSITA. What dove shall I look for, anxiously,
  To bring me news of your coming?
NEPHEW. The dove that stands for my loyalty.
ROSITA. Then I for the two of us
  Will embroider the whitest sheets.
NEPHEW. In Jesus's name, his diamond crown,
  The red carnation of his side and feet,
  I promise I shall come back again.
ROSITA. God go with you, cousin!
NEPHEW. God be with you, till we meet again!

They embrace in the 'vis-à-vis'. The piano is heard distantly. The NEPHEW *leaves.* ROSITA *is left weeping. The* UNCLE *appears and crosses the stage towards the greenhouse. When she sees her uncle,* ROSITA *picks up the rose book which is nearby.*

UNCLE. What were you doing?
ROSITA. Nothing.
UNCLE. Reading?
ROSITA. Yes.

The UNCLE *leaves.* ROSITA *reads aloud from the book.*

She opens in the morning,
Her colour the deepest red.
Afraid of being burnt by her,
The dew has quickly fled.

At noon her petals, open wide,
Have all the firmness of coral.
The sun looks down to gaze upon
The splendour of its rival.

When birds take to the branches
To announce the approach of sleep,
And evening begins to slip
Into the sea's azure deep.

Then her red grows deadly pale,
Like a cheek by sorrow torn,
And night, approaching softly,
Blows on a metal horn.

The stars advance across the sky,
The wind no longer calls,
As on the edge of darkness,
Her petals begin to fall.

Curtain.

Act Two

A room in DOÑA ROSITA'*s house. The garden in the background.*

MR X. I shall always be a man of this century.

UNCLE. The century we've just begun will be pure materialism.

MR X. But far more progressive than the last one. My friend, Mr Longoria, from Madrid, has just bought a motor car. He can hurtle along in it at the incredible speed of eighteen miles an hour. And the Shah of Persia – a really pleasant man – has bought himself a twenty-four horsepower Panhard Levasson.

UNCLE. I'd like to know where everyone's going in such a hurry. You've heard what's happened in the Paris–Madrid rally. They had to abandon it. All the competitors were dead before they got to Bordeaux.

MR X. Count Zbronsky, killed in the accident. And Marcel Renault, or Renol – it is and may be pronounced either way – killed as well. Both martyrs of science! Both will be given the highest honour the day the religion of the positive truly dawns! Renol I knew well. Poor Marcello!

UNCLE. You won't convince me. (*He sits down*).

MR X (*a foot on the chair and playing with his cane*). I shall do so dazzlingly, though a teacher of Political Economy can't really discuss things with a rose-grower. But in this day and age, take my word, neither quietism nor obscurantism can make the slightest headway. Nowadays, the way ahead is opened up for us by a Jean-Baptiste Say or Se – it is and may be pronounced either

115

way – or a Count Leo Tolstwa, vulgarly Tolstoy, as elegant in form as he is profound in concept. I feel myself to be in the living *polis*. I am not a supporter of *natura naturata*.

UNCLE. Everyone lives his daily life as best he can or best knows how.

MR X. Of course, this Earth of ours is a very mediocre planet, and one must give a hand to civilization. Now, if Santos Dumont, instead of studying comparative meteorology, had devoted his life to the cultivation of roses, the navigable aerostat would be in the bosom of Brahma.

UNCLE (*annoyed*). Botany is a science too!

MR X (*disparagingly*). Ah, yes. But an applied science: to study the juices of the fragrant Anthemis or the rhubarb, or the great Pulsatilla, or the narcotic of the Datura Stramonium.

UNCLE (*innocently*). Are you interested in those plants?

MR X. I do not have sufficient experience as far as they are concerned. What interests me is culture, which is quite a different matter. Voila! (*Pause.*) And ... Rosita?

UNCLE. Rosita? (*Pause – calling out.*) Rosita! ...

VOICE (*off*). She's not here.

MR X. Ah, what a pity!

UNCLE. Such a pity! It's her saint's day, so she'll have gone out to say her forty prayers.

MR X. Please give her this pendant on my behalf. It's a mother-of-pearl Eiffel Tower over two doves bearing in their beaks the wheel of industry.

UNCLE. She will be grateful to you.

MR X. I was tempted to give her a small silver cannon through whose mouth one could see the Virgin of Lourdes, or Lordes, or a buckle for a belt composed of a serpent and four dragonflies. I chose the first. Seemed to me to be in better taste.

UNCLE. Many thanks.

MR X. Delighted by your warm welcome!

UNCLE. Thank you so much.

MR X. My humble respects to your dear wife.

UNCLE. Many thanks again.

MR X. And my humble respects to your enchanting dear niece. I wish her the best of fortune on her saint's feast day.

UNCLE. A thousand thanks.

MR X. Consider me your obedient servant.

UNCLE. A million thanks.

MR X. I assure you once more . . .

UNCLE. Thank you, thank you, thank you . . .

MR X. Goodbye for now. (*He leaves.*)

UNCLE (*calling after him*). Thank you, thank you, thank you.

HOUSEKEEPER (*enters laughing*). I don't know how you have the patience. Between this gentleman and the other one – that Mr Confucius Montes de Oca, baptized in lodge number forty-three – the day will come the house will be burned to the ground.

UNCLE. I've told you before I don't like you eavesdropping.

HOUSEKEEPER. Well, that's what's called being ungrateful. I *was* behind the door, I admit that, sir, but it wasn't to listen – only to put a broom upside down so that the gentleman would leave!

AUNT (*entering*). Has he gone?

UNCLE (*leaving*). This very minute.

HOUSEKEEPER. Is *he* courting Rosita too?

AUNT. Why mention courting? You obviously don't know Rosita!

HOUSEKEEPER. But I do know her suitors.

AUNT. My niece is engaged.

HOUSEKEEPER. Oh, don't make me say it! Don't make

me say it! Don't make me say it! Don't make me say it!

AUNT. Well, don't say it!

HOUSEKEEPER. Does it seem right to you for a man to go off and leave for fifteen years a woman who's the cream on the butter. She ought to get married. My hands are aching from putting away tablecloths of Marseilles lace, embroidered bed-sets, tablemats, and gauze bedspreads with embossed flowers. She ought to be using them, wearing them out, but she doesn't seem to realize that time is passing. She'll have hair like silver and she'll still be sewing satin bands on the ruffles of her honeymoon nightdress.

AUNT. But why do you get involved in things that don't concern you?

HOUSEKEEPER (*astonished*). I don't get involved. I *am* involved!

AUNT. I'm sure she's happy.

HOUSEKEEPER. She thinks she is. Yesterday she had me with her all day long at the entrance to the circus. She insisted that one of the puppeteers looked like her cousin.

AUNT. Did he?

HOUSEKEEPER. He was as good-looking as a young priest singing his first Mass. Your nephew would have given anything to have that waist, that white throat, that moustache. He wasn't a bit like him. There aren't any good-looking men in your family.

AUNT. Oh, thank you very much!

HOUSEKEEPER. They are all short and a bit round-shouldered.

AUNT. Go on with you!

HOUSEKEEPER. It's the honest truth, madam. What happened is that Rosita found the acrobat very good-looking. So did I, and you would too. But she's always thinking that fiancé of hers is the same. Sometimes I'd like to throw a shoe at her head. She's going to have cow's eyes from so much staring into space.

AUNT. Alright, but that's enough. It's as well and good for the clown to speak, but not to bark.

HOUSEKEEPER. You aren't going to tell me that I don't love her!

AUNT. Sometimes I think you don't.

HOUSEKEEPER. I'd take the bread from my mouth and the blood from my veins if she wanted them.

AUNT (*strongly*). Oh, very fine-sounding, sugar-coated words!

HOUSEKEEPER (*strongly*). And deeds! I've proved it! By my actions! I love her more than you!

AUNT. That's a lie!

HOUSEKEEPER (*strongly*). It's the truth!

AUNT. Don't raise your voice to me!

HOUSEKEEPER (*loudly*). That's what my tongue is for!

AUNT. Be quiet, you ill-bred woman!

HOUSEKEEPER. Forty years I've been in your service.

AUNT (*almost crying*). You are dismissed!

HOUSEKEEPER (*very loudly*). Thank God I shan't have to see you any more!

AUNT (*crying*). Get out! At once!

HOUSEKEEPER (*starting to cry*). I'm going!

She goes to the door in tears. As she goes she drops something. Both women are crying. Pause.

AUNT (*wiping away her tears, speaking gently*). What have you dropped?

HOUSEKEEPER (*crying*). A Louis the Fifteenth thermometer case.

AUNT. Really?

HOUSEKEEPER. Yes, madam. (*Weeping.*)

AUNT. Let me see.

HOUSEKEEPER (*approaching*). It's for Rosita's saint's day.

AUNT (*sniffing*). It's really lovely.

HOUSEKEEPER (*in a tearful voice*). In the middle of the velvet there's a fountain made out of real shells. Over the fountain there's a wire arbour with green roses. The water in the basin is a cluster of blue sequins, and the jet is the thermometer itself. The pools of water here and there are painted in oil and there's a nightingale drinking, embroidered in gold thread. I wanted one that you could wind up so it would play a tune, but there wasn't one.

AUNT. Oh, dear!

HOUSEKEEPER. Still, it doesn't *have* to sing. We've got real birds in the garden.

AUNT. Of course we have! (*Pause.*) Why have you gone to so much trouble?

HOUSEKEEPER (*crying*). Everything I've got is for Rosita.

AUNT. You really do love her more than anyone!

HOUSEKEEPER. But not as much as you!

AUNT. Yes. You've given her your blood.

HOUSEKEEPER. You've sacrificed your life for her.

AUNT. I've done it out of duty, but you out of generosity.

HOUSEKEEPER (*louder*). No, you haven't!

AUNT. You've proved that you love her more than anyone.

HOUSEKEEPER. I've done what anyone in my place would have done. I'm just a servant. You pay me and I work for you.

AUNT. We've always regarded you as one of the family.

HOUSEKEEPER. An ordinary servant who gives what she has, that's all I am.

AUNT. What do you mean that's all you are?

HOUSEKEEPER. Am I anything more?

AUNT (*annoyed*). You aren't allowed to say that here. I'm going, so as not to hear you.

HOUSEKEEPER (*annoyed*). So am I!

They go out through different doors. As the AUNT *goes out, she bumps into the* UNCLE.

UNCLE. With you two living on top of each other, the softest lace becomes a sharp thorn.

AUNT. It's just that she always wants to have her own way.

UNCLE. Don't tell me! I know it all by heart . . . Still, you can't do without her. Yesterday I could hear you giving her all the details of our current bank account. You don't know your place. It doesn't seem to me the ideal topic of conversation for a servant.

AUNT. She's not a servant!

UNCLE (*gently*). Alright, alright. I don't want to argue the point.

AUNT. Oh, come! You can say whatever you like to me.

UNCLE. Of course I can! But I prefer to keep quiet.

AUNT. Even though your resentment's bottled up inside?

UNCLE. What's the point of saying anything at this stage? For a bit of peace and quiet I'd rather make my bed, clean my suits with soap, or change the carpets in my room.

AUNT. It isn't fair to regard yourself as superior, neglected by the rest of us, when the fact of the matter is that everything in the house has to take second place to your comfort and your likes!

UNCLE (*sweetly*). It's the other way round, my girl.

AUNT (*seriously*). I mean everything. Instead of making lace, I prune the plants. What do you do for me?

UNCLE. Oh, come! There comes a moment when people who've lived together for years find reasons to be bad-tempered and touchy about the smallest things. It's their way of putting a bit of life and spark into something that's really dead. We never had these conversations when we were twenty.

AUNT. No. When we were twenty the windows used to shatter . . .

UNCLE. And the cold was a toy that amused us . . .

ROSITA *appears. She is dressed in pink. The styles have changed from the leg-o'-mutton sleeves of 1900. Her skirt is bell-shaped. She crosses the stage quickly with a pair of scissors in her hand. She stops in the centre of the stage . . .*

ROSITA. Has the postman been?

UNCLE. Has he been?

AUNT. I don't know. (*Calling out.*) Has the postman been? No. Not yet.

ROSITA. He always comes at this time.

UNCLE. He should have been here by now.

AUNT. Very often he's held up.

ROSITA. Only the other day I met him playing hop-scotch with three children, and a big pile of letters on the floor.

AUNT. He'll be here soon.

ROSITA. Call me when he comes. (*She goes out quickly.*)

UNCLE. What are you going to do with the scissors?

ROSITA. Cut some roses.

UNCLE (*surprised*). What? Who's given you permission?

AUNT. I have. It's her saint's day.

ROSITA. I want to put some in the window-boxes and in the vase in the front hall.

UNCLE. Whenever you cut a rose, it's as if you've cut off one of my fingers. I know it's the same (*Looking at his wife*). I don't want to argue about it. I know they don't last long. (*The* HOUSEKEEPER *enters.*) That's how the song goes – the Waltz of the Roses, one of the most beautiful songs we have. I really can't hide my feelings when I see roses in a vase. (*He leaves.*)

ROSITA (*to the* HOUSEKEEPER). Has the post come?

HOUSEKEEPER. The only thing roses are good for is to make rooms pretty.

ROSITA (*annoyed*). I asked you if the post's come.

HOUSEKEEPER (*annoyed*). Do you think I keep the letters to myself when they arrive?

AUNT. Go on now. Cut the flowers.

ROSITA. In this house there's a drop of bitterness with everything.

HOUSEKEEPER. Oh, yes. We find arsenic in all the corners. (*She leaves.*)

AUNT. Are you happy?

ROSITA. I don't know.

AUNT. What does that mean?

ROSITA. When I don't see people I'm happy, but since I have to see them . . .

AUNT. Of course you do! I don't like the kind of life you are leading. Your fiancé doesn't want you to spend all your time at home. He's always telling me in his letters that you should go out.

ROSITA. It's just that in the street I can see that time is passing and I don't want to lose my illusions. They've built another new house in the little square. I don't want to be reminded that time is passing me by!

AUNT. Of course you don't! I've told you often enough to write to your cousin and marry someone else here. You're a lively girl. I know there are lots of men in love with you, young ones and older ones.

ROSITA. Oh, Aunt. My roots have gone deep – deep down into my feelings. If it weren't for seeing other people, I'd think it was only a week ago that he went away. I wait as if it were still the very first day. Anyway, what's a year, or two years, or five? (*A little bell is heard.*) It's the post.

AUNT. I wonder what he's sent.

HOUSEKEEPER (*entering*). It's those awful old maids.

AUNT. Holy Mary!

ROSITA. Ask them in.

HOUSEKEEPER. The mother and the three girls. All show on the outside and only a few stale crumbs to keep them going . . . I'd give them a good spanking across their . . . ! (*She goes out.*)

The three pretentious girls enter with their mother. The THREE SPINSTERS *wear huge hats with tasteless feathers, ridiculous dresses, gloves to the elbow with bracelets over them, and fans dangling from long chains. The* MOTHER *wears a faded black dress and a hat with old purple ribbons.*

MOTHER (*kissing* ROSITA.) Happy birthday!

ROSITA. Thank you. (*She kisses the* SPINSTERS *in turn.*) Love! Charity! Mercy!

FIRST SPINSTER. Happy birthday!

SECOND SPINSTER. Happy birthday!

THIRD SPINSTER. Happy birthday!

AUNT (*to the* MOTHER). How are your feet?

MOTHER. Worse all the time. If it weren't for my girls, I'd be stuck at home. (*They sit down.*)

AUNT. Have you tried rubbing them with lavender?

FIRST SPINSTER. Every night.

SECOND SPINSTER. And the boiled mallows.

AUNT. That cures every kind of rheumatism.

Pause.

MOTHER. How is your husband?

AUNT. Quite well, thank you.

Pause.

MOTHER. Still with his roses?

AUNT. Still with his roses.

THIRD SPINSTER. Oh, flowers are so pretty!

SECOND SPINSTER. We've got a Saint Francis rosebush in a pot!

ROSITA. But the Saint Francis rose doesn't have a scent.

FIRST SPINSTER. Hardly any.

MOTHER. My favourites are the syringas.

THIRD SPINSTER. And violets are pretty too.

Pause.

MOTHER. Well, girls. Have you brought the card?

THIRD SPINSTER. Yes. It's a little girl dressed in pink who's also a barometer. The monk with his cape is much too common now. The little girl's skirts are made of very thin paper and, according to whether it's damp or not, they open and close.

ROSITA (*reading*). In the meadow one morning
The nightingale's singing.
Its song proclaiming
Rosita's a darling.

You really shouldn't have!

AUNT. Oh, how tasteful!

MOTHER. I've never lacked taste! Only money!

FIRST SPINSTER. Mamma!

SECOND SPINSTER. Mamma!

THIRD SPINSTER. Mamma!

MOTHER. Now girls, I'm among friends here. There's no one can hear us. You know perfectly well that since my poor husband was taken from me I've performed real miracles in order to manage on a pension. I fancy I can still hear the father of these girls when, generous gentleman that he was, he used to tell me: 'Henrietta, spend, spend, spend. I'm earning decent money now.' Ah well, those days are gone! But even so, we've managed to keep our position in society. What agony I've gone through, madam, so that my girls shouldn't be deprived of hats! I've shed many a tear, sighed many a sigh on account of a ribbon or an arrangement of curls! Those feathers and wires have cost me many a sleepless night!

THIRD SPINSTER. Mamma ... !

MOTHER. But it's the truth, my child. We can't spend at all beyond our means. Many's the time I say to them: 'Now what do you really want, dear girls? An egg for breakfast or a chair when you promenade?' They all reply together: 'A chair.'

THIRD SPINSTER. Mamma, don't go on so. The whole of Granada's heard it.

MOTHER. But then, what else could they say? We may have to eat potatoes or a bunch of grapes, but we've still got our Mongolian cape, or a painted parasol, or a poplinette blouse with all the trimmings. There's just no alternative. Even so, it's such an ordeal! My eyes fill with tears when I see them competing with girls who have money.

SECOND SPINSTER. Aren't you going to the park today, Rosita?

ROSITA. No.

THIRD SPINSTER. We always meet up with the Ponce de León girls, or the Herrastis of the daughters of the Baroness of Saint Matilda of the Papal Benediction. All the best in Granada.

MOTHER. Of course, they were at Heaven's Gate School together. (*Pause.*)

AUNT (*rising*). What would you like to eat? (*They all rise.*)

MOTHER. You have the most delicate hands when it comes to puff pastries with pine nuts!

FIRST SPINSTER (*to* ROSITA). Have you had any news?

ROSITA. The last letter suggested there might be. I'm waiting to see what this one brings.

THIRD SPINSTER. Have you finished the set with the valencienne lace?

ROSITA. Of course! And another one of nainsook with moiré butterflies.

SECOND SPINSTER. The day you marry you'll have the best trousseau in the world.

ROSITA. Oh, I still think it's not enough. They say that men get tired of a girl if they always see her dressed the same.

HOUSEKEEPER (*entering*). The Ayola girls are here. The

photographer's daughters!

AUNT. You really mean the Misses Ayola.

HOUSEKEEPER. The big-shot daughters of the high and mighty Ayola, photographer to his Majesty the King, winner of the gold medal at the Madrid Exhibition! (*Leaves.*)

AUNT. One has to put up with her; but there are times when she sets my nerves on edge. (*The* SPINSTERS *are with* ROSITA *looking at some linens*). Servants are impossible.

MOTHER. And cheeky! I have a girl who cleans the flat for us in the afternoons. She was earning what they've always earned: a peseta a month plus the leftovers, which isn't bad in times like these. Well, the other day she suddenly came out with a demand for five pestas, and I just can't manage it!

AUNT. I don't know where it's all going to end.

The AYOLA GIRLS *enter and greet* ROSITA *happily. They are richly dressed in the greatly exaggerated style of the period.*

ROSITA. Do you know each other?

FIRST AYOLA. Only by sight.

ROSITA. The Misses Ayola, Mrs Scarpini and her daughters.

SECOND AYOLA. We see them sitting when we promenade. (*They try to conceal laughter.*)

ROSITA. Please take a seat. (*The* SPINSTERS *sit.*)

AUNT (*to the* AYOLA GIRLS). Would you care for a sweet?

SECOND AYOLA. Oh, no! We ate just a little while ago. To tell the truth, I had four eggs with tomato sauce. I could hardly get up from the chair.

FIRST AYOLA. How amusing!

They laugh. Pause. The AYOLAS *begin an uncontrollable laughter which communicates itself to* ROSITA. ROSITA *tries not to laugh. The* SPINSTERS *and the* MOTHER *are serious. Pause.*

AUNT. What children!

MOTHER. To be young!

AUNT. Such a happy time!

ROSITA (*walking about the stage as if arranging things*). Oh, please be quiet! (*They stop laughing.*)

AUNT (*to the* THIRD SPINSTER): Why don't you play the piano for us?

THIRD SPINSTER. I don't practise much. I've got too much needlework to do.

ROSITA. It's a very long time since I heard you play.

MOTHER. If it weren't for me, her fingers would be as stiff as pokers. But I'm always telling her – 'Practise! Practise!'

SECOND SPINSTER. Since poor Daddy died she doesn't want to play. He loved to listen!

SECOND AYOLA. I remember sometimes the tears would run down his face.

FIRST SPINSTER. When she played Popper's 'Tarantella'.

SECOND SPINSTER. And the 'Virgin's Prayer'.

MOTHER. With so much feeling!

> The AYOLAS, *who have been restraining themselves, burst out laughing. Great peals of laughter.* ROSITA, *with her back to the* SPINSTERS, *laughs too but controls herself.*

AUNT. What girls!

FIRST AYOLA. We are laughing because, before we arrived . . .

SECOND AYOLA. She tripped and almost did a somersault . . .

FIRST AYOLA. And I . . . (*They laugh.*)

> The SPINSTERS *pretend to smile in a somewhat weary and sad manner.*

MOTHER. Well, we must be off.

AUNT. Oh, you mustn't go yet!

ROSITA (*to everybody*). Let's be thankful that you didn't fall. (*To the* HOUSEKEEPER.) Bring the Saint Kathleen's Bones.

THIRD SPINSTER. They are very rich!

MOTHER. Last year someone gave us a whole pound.

The HOUSEKEEPER *enters with the Bones.*

HOUSEKEEPER. Titbits for fine people! (*to* ROSITA.) The postman's coming through the poplars.

ROSITA. Wait for him at the door.

FIRST AYOLA. I'm not hungry. I'd rather have an anisette.

ROSITA. You were always fond of the bottle!

FIRST AYOLA. When I was six I used to come here and Rosita's fiancé got me used to drinking. Do you remember, Rosita?

ROSITA (*seriously*). No!

SECOND AYOLA. Rosita and her fiancé used to teach me my A, B, C . . . How many years ago was it?

AUNT. Fifteen!

FIRST AYOLA. I've almost forgotten what your fiancé looked like.

SECOND AYOLA. Didn't he have a mark on his lip?

ROSITA. A mark? Aunty, did he have a mark on his lip?

AUNT. But don't you remember, child? It was the one thing that spoilt his face.

ROSITA. But it wasn't a scar. It was a burn, rather red. Scars are deep things.

FIRST AYOLA. My wish is for Rosita to get married!

ROSITA. Oh, good Lord!

SECOND AYOLA. Don't be silly. I want you to too!

ROSITA. But why?

FIRST AYOLA. So we can go to a wedding. I'm getting married as soon as I can!

AUNT. Child!

FIRST AYOLA. To anyone! I don't want to be an old maid.

SECOND AYOLA. I agree entirely.

AUNT (*to the* MOTHER). What's your opinion?

FIRST AYOLA. And if I'm Rosita's friend, it's because she has a sweetheart! Women without sweethearts are faded, eaten-up inside, and all of them . . . (*Noticing the* SPINSTERS.) . . . well, not all . . . some of them . . . Well, anyway, they are all boiling up inside!

AUNT. Now that's quite enough!

MOTHER. Pay no attention!

FIRST SPINSTER. There are lots of girls who don't marry because they don't want to.

SECOND AYOLA. I don't believe a word of it.

FIRST SPINSTER (*peevishly*). I know it for a fact!

SECOND AYOLA. A girl who doesn't want to get married doesn't powder her face, doesn't wear falsies, and doesn't sit on her balcony all day and night eying the passers-by.

SECOND SPINSTER. Perhaps such a girl simply likes to take the air!

ROSITA. What a silly conversation this is!

They all laugh in a forced manner.

AUNT. Very well, why don't we play a little?

MOTHER. Come along, child!

THIRD SPINSTER (*getting up*). But what shall I play?

SECOND AYOLA. Play 'Viva Frascuelo'!

SECOND SPINSTER. The barcarolle from 'The Frigate Numancia'.

ROSITA. And why not 'What the Flowers Say'?

MOTHER. Oh yes! 'What the Flowers Say'! (*To the* AUNT.) Have you heard her perform it? She recites and plays at the same time. Sheer beauty!

THIRD SPINSTER. I can also recite: 'The dark swallows will return, to build their nests in your balcony'.

FIRST AYOLA. That's too sad.

FIRST SPINSTER. Sad is beautiful too.

AUNT. Come along then! Come along!

THIRD SPINSTER (*at the piano*).
Mother, take me to the fields
As day begins to break,
To see the flowers open
And the branches start to wake.
A thousand flowers whisper
To a thousand love-struck maidens,
And the fountain tells a story
That the nightingale keeps hidden.

ROSITA. The rose had opened quickly
In the early-morning light;
As red as fresh-spilt blood,
It had put the dew to flight.
So dazzling upon its stem,
Its fire burnt the air;
How tall it stood, how splendid!
Its petals bright and fair.

THIRD SPINSTER. 'Only on you do I set my eyes',
The heliotrope would sigh.
'And I can never love you',
Is the basil-flower's cry.
The violet says, 'I'm timid.'
The white rose says, 'I'm cold.'
The jasmine says, 'I'm faithful.'
The carnation boasts, 'I'm bold.'

SECOND SPINSTER. The hyacinth means bitterness,
The passion-flower pain.

FIRST SPINSTER. The lily is eternal hope,
The mustard flower disdain.

AUNT. The gardenia says, 'I am your friend.'
'I trust you', the passion flower.
The honeysuckle soothes you,
The evergreen kills for sure.

MOTHER. Evergreen that stands for death,
　Clasped by hands that pray,
　How fine you seem when the soft breeze
　Weeps on a funeral day.

ROSITA. The rose's petals are open wide,
　But evening advances,
　And the sad sound of falling snow
　Is heavy on the branches.
　When shadows come and nightingales sing,
　Recounting their sad tale,
　Like one who's overwhelmed by grief,
　She grows white and pale.
　When night descends, announcing itself
　On its great metallic horn,
　When the breeze sleeps on the mountain-top,
　And the winds no longer moan.
　Then it is that her death begins,
　And she longs to see the dawn.

THIRD SPINSTER.
　Dead flowers weep in your long, soft hair,
　Some of them sharp as knives.
　Others are like ice or fire,
　Matching a maiden's sighs.

FIRST SPINSTER. The flowers have a language,
　A meaning of their own.
　Who can understand it?
　Only those by love overthrown.

ROSITA. The willow-herb speaks of jealousy,
　The dahlia of disdain,
　The fleur-de-lis of laughter,
　The gardenia of love's pain.
　Yellow flowers all mean hate,
　Scarlet speaks of passion's heat,
　White foretells a bridal gown
　And blue a fatal winding-sheet.

THIRD SPINSTER. Mother, take me to the fields
  As day begins to break,
  To see the flowers open
  And the branches start to wake.

  The piano plays a last scale and stops.

AUNT. Isn't that beautiful!

MOTHER. They know the language of the fan, the language of gloves, the language of stamps, and the language of the hours. I get goosepimples when they sing the one that goes:

  Twelve o'clock strikes the world over,
  Echoing harsh and clear,
  Think well on it now, sinner,
  The hour of death draws near.

FIRST AYOLA. Oh, what a hideous song!

MOTHER. And then there's the other one:

  At one o'clock are we born,
  Tra, la, la.
  To be born at such an hour,
  Tra, la, la,
  Is to open these eyes of ours,
  Tra, la, la,
  In a meadow of beautiful flowers,
  flowers, flowers. Tra, la, la.

SECOND AYOLA (*to her sister*). I think the old lady's had a drop too much. (*To the* MOTHER.) Would you care for another glass?

MOTHER. With the utmost pleasure and the best will in the world, as they used to say in my time.

  ROSITA *has been watching for the postman's arrival.*

HOUSEKEEPER. The postman!

  General excitement.

AUNT. And just at the right time!

THIRD SPINSTER. He must have picked today!

MOTHER. How considerate of him!

SECOND AYOLA. Open the letter!

FIRST AYOLA. It would be more appropriate for you to read it alone, just in case there's something rather daring.

MOTHER. Heavens!

ROSITA *leaves with the letter.*

FIRST AYOLA. A love-letter isn't a prayer book, you know.

THIRD SPINSTER. It's a prayer book of love.

SECOND AYOLA. Oh, what an exquisite comparison!

The AYOLAS *laugh.*

FIRST AYOLA. You can tell she's never received one.

MOTHER (*forcefully*). Fortunately for her!

FIRST AYOLA. So it's her look-out!

AUNT (*to the* HOUSEKEEPER *who starts to go out to* ROSITA). Where are you going?

HOUSEKEEPER. Can't I put one foot in front of the other?

AUNT. Just leave her be!

ROSITA (*entering*). Aunt! Aunt!

AUNT. What is it, child?

ROSITA (*excitedly*). Oh, Aunt!

FIRST AYOLA. What is it?

THIRD SPINSTER. Tell us!

SECOND AYOLA. What is it?

HOUSEKEEPER. Speak!

AUNT. Out with it!

MOTHER. A glass of water!

SECOND AYOLA. Come on!

FIRST AYOLA. Quickly!

Excitement and flurry.

ROSITA (*in a choking voice*). He's decided to marry ...

(*Alarm on all their faces.*) . . . to marry me, because he can't wait any more, but . . .

SECOND AYOLA (*embracing her*). Hooray! What happiness!

FIRST AYOLA. Let me hug you!

AUNT. Let her speak!

ROSITA (*more calmly*). But he can't come at present, so the wedding will be by proxy and he will come later on.

FIRST SPINSTER. Congratulations!

MOTHER (*almost weeping*). May God give you the happiness you deserve!

She embraces ROSITA.

HOUSEKEEPER. And what's this 'by proxy'? What's it mean?

ROSITA. Nothing. Someone represents the goom at the ceremony.

HOUSEKEEPER. And what else?

ROSITA. Just that a girl's married then!

HOUSEKEEPER. What about the nights?

ROSITA. Heavens!

FIRST AYOLA. There's a point! What about the nights?

AUNT. Girls!

HOUSEKEEPER. He should come in person to marry you! 'By proxy!' I've never heard of it. The sheets trembling with the cold and the bride's nightdress still in the bottom of the trunk! Madam, don't ever let proxies into this house! (*They all laugh.*) Madam, I can't abide proxies!

ROSITA. But he'll soon be here himself. It's one more proof of just how much he loves me!

HOUSEKEEPER. And I say: Let him come and take you by the arm. And let him stir the sugar in your coffee and taste it first to see if it burns!

Laughter. The UNCLE *enters with a rose.*

ROSITA. Uncle!

UNCLE. I heard everything and, almost without thinking,
I cut the only Rosa Mutabile in the greenhouse. It was
still red.

By noon her petals open wide
Have all the firmness of coral.

ROSITA. The sun looks down to gaze upon
The splendour of its rival.

UNCLE. If I'd waited two hours more, I would have given
it to you white.

ROSITA. Like the whiteness of a dove,
Like the sea's sad smiling,
Like the white, white coldness
Of a cheek marked by grieving.

UNCLE. But at the moment it still has the flame of youth.

AUNT. Husband, a little drink with me! It's the right
day for it.

Excitement. The THIRD SPINSTER *goes to the piano and
plays a polka.* ROSITA *is looking at the rose. The* FIRST
and SECOND SPINSTERS *dance with the* AYOLAS
and sing.

I saw you a young woman
On the sea-shore standing.
Your sweet, sad manner
Was the cause of my longing.
That delicate sweetness
Of my fatal illusion,
In the light of the moon
Was sudden confusion.

The AUNT *and* UNCLE *dance.* ROSITA *goes to the pair
formed by the* SECOND SPINSTER *and the* AYOLA. *She
dances with the* SPINSTER. *On seeing the old couple dance, the*
AYOLA *claps her hands. The* HOUSEKEEPER *enters and
joins in.*

Curtain.

Act Three

A small sitting room with green shutters opening on to the garden.
The stage is silent. A clock strikes six in the evening. The
HOUSEKEEPER *crosses the stage carrying a box and a suitcase.*
Ten years have passed. The AUNT *appears and sits on a low*
chair in the centre of the stage. Silence. The clock strikes six once
more. Pause.

HOUSEKEEPER (*entering*). Six o'clock for the second time.

AUNT. Where's Rosita?

HOUSEKEEPER. Up there in the tower. Where were you?

AUNT. In the greenhouse, getting the flowerpots together.

HOUSEKEEPER. I haven't seen you all morning.

AUNT. Since my husband died, the house is so empty it
seems twice as big. We even have to go around looking
for each other. Some nights, when I cough in my room,
I can hear it echoing as if I were in a church.

HOUSEKEEPER. The house is really far too big.

AUNT. Oh, if he were only still alive, with his vision, with
all his talent . . . ! (*Almost weeping.*)

HOUSEKEEPER (*singing*). La, la, tra, la, la . . . No, madam,
crying I won't allow! It's six years since he died, and
I don't want you to be like you were on the first day.
We've cried enough for him! Our steps must be firm
and sure, madam! Let the sun shine in the dark corners!
He can wait for us for years yet while we go on cutting
our roses!

AUNT (*rising*). I'm very old. And we have a great burden
to carry.

HOUSEKEEPER. It'll be alright. I'm old too, you know!

137

AUNT. I wish I were as old as you!

HOUSEKEEPER. There's not much difference between us, but I've worked hard, so my joints are well oiled. Your legs have gone thin and stiff from too much sitting around!

AUNT. Do you really think that I haven't worked?

HOUSEKEEPER. Only with the tips of your fingers – with thread, flowers, jams. I've worked with my back, with my knees, with my fingernails.

AUNT. So, running a house isn't really working?

HOUSEKEEPER. It's much harder scrubbing floors.

AUNT. Well, I don't want to argue.

HOUSEKEEPER. Why not? It helps to pass the time. Come on! Answer me back! We've lost our tongues! In the old days we used to shout at each other – 'What about this? What about that? Where's the custard? Get on with the ironing!' . . .

AUNT. I'm quite resigned now . . . soup one day, the next fried breadcrumbs. My little glass of water, my rosary in my purse . . . I would wait for death with dignity . . . But when I think of Rosita!

HOUSEKEEPER. That's what really hurts!

AUNT (angrily). When I think of the wrong that's been done to her, of all the time she's been deceived, of the falseness of that man's heart! He wasn't one of our family. He could never be one of us! I wish I were twenty years old so that I could take a boat to Tucumán! I'd take a whip to him . . .

HOUSEKEEPER (breaking in). . . . and a sword to cut off his head and crush it with two stones and chop off the hand that made false promises and wrote so many lying love-letters!

AUNT. He should be made to pay with blood for what has cost blood, even if it were all my blood! And then . . .

HOUSEKEEPER. . . . . Scatter his ashes on the sea!

AUNT. Bring him back to life and give him to Rosita! Then I could breathe easily again, knowing the family honour was restored.

HOUSEKEEPER. You have to admit I was right about him.

AUNT. So you were!

HOUSEKEEPER. He found and married the rich girl he was looking for, but he should have told us there and then. Who's going to want this woman now? She's too old! Oh, madam, couldn't we send him a poisoned letter that would kill him as soon as he opened it?

AUNT. Don't be silly! He's been married for eight years, and it was only last month that the wretch could write to tell me the truth! I could tell by his letters that there was something – the power of attorney that never came, a kind of hesitation . . . He didn't dare tell the truth until now, after his father's death! And this poor child . . .

HOUSEKEEPER. Shh . . .

AUNT (*changing the subject*). And take the two pots out.

ROSITA *enters. She wears a light pink dress in the style of 1910. She has long curls. She looks a good deal older.*

HOUSEKEEPER. Child!

ROSITA. What are you doing?

HOUSEKEEPER. Oh, having a bit of a grumble. Where are you going?

ROSITA. To the greenhouse. Have they taken the plants?

AUNT. There are still a few there.

ROSITA *leaves. The two women wipe away their tears.*

HOUSEKEEPER. Is this all there is? You sitting there and me sitting here? And both of us waiting to die? . . . Isn't there any law? Haven't we got the courage to pulverize him?

AUNT. Hush! Leave it now!

HOUSEKEEPER. I haven't got the patience to put up with all this without my heart scampering about inside me like a dog that's being chased. When I buried my husband, I was truly sad, but deep down I was happy . . . no, not happy . . . glad to see that it wasn't me being buried. When I buried my daughter – you'll know what I mean – when I buried that little girl, it was as if they were trampling on my insides. But, even so, the dead are dead. They are gone, the door closes, and we must live! But this situation with Rosita is the worst of all. It's like loving someone and not being able to find him; like crying and not knowing who you are crying for; like sighing for someone you know doesn't deserve it. It's an open wound that trickles a thread of blood endlessly, and there's no one, no one in the world to bring the cotton wool, the bandages, or the precious pieces of ice.

AUNT. What do you want me to do?

HOUSEKEEPER. Let the current take us.

AUNT. Everything turns its back on old age.

HOUSEKEEPER. While I've got my strength, you'll lack for nothing.

AUNT (*pause. She speaks quietly, with a sense of shame*). Woman, I can't go on paying you your monthly wage. You'll have to leave us.

HOUSEKEEPER. Wheee! Listen to that wind blowing through the window! Wheee! Or am I going deaf? . . . And why do I feel the urge to sing? Like the children coming out of school! (*Children's voices are heard.*) Can you hear them, madam? Oh, madam, my madam always! (*Embracing her.*)

AUNT. Listen to me!

HOUSEKEEPER. I'm going to make a casserole of mackerel flavoured with fennel.

AUNT. You must listen!

HOUSEKEEPER. And a snow mountain! I'm going to make you a snow custard covered with coloured sugar . . .

AUNT. But woman! . . .

HOUSEKEEPER. I am! . . . Why, it's Don Martín! Don Martín, come in! Come in! Amuse my mistress for a while!

The HOUSEKEEPER *leaves quickly.* DON MARTÍN *enters. He is an old man with red hair. He walks with a crutch which supports a crippled leg. He is a dignified, aristocratic man, with a marked air of sadness.*

AUNT. Don Martín, a sight for sore eyes!

DON MARTÍN. Is the day fixed for moving?

AUNT. It's today!

DON MARTÍN. So you really are going?

AUNT. The new house isn't as good as this. But it has a nice view and a small patio with two fig trees where we can grow some flowers.

DON MARTÍN. Much better, much better!

AUNT. And how are you?

DON MARTÍN. Oh, the same old life! I've just given my class on Rhetoric. Like being in Hell itself! It was a wonderful topic: 'Concept and Definition of Harmony'. But the children couldn't care less! What children they are! They can see I'm disabled, so they do have a bit of respect: maybe the odd drawing-pin on the seat of my chair, or a paper doll stuck on my back. As for my colleagues, they do the most terrible things to them. They are all the children of rich parents, so they pay and you can't punish them. The headmaster's always telling us that. Why, yesterday they insisted on saying that poor Mr Canito, the new geography teacher, was wearing a corset, just because his waist's on the narrow side. Anyway, when he was alone in the patio, the bullies and the boarders got together, stripped him

from the waist up, tied him to one of the pillars in the
corridor, and poured a jug of water on him from the
balcony above.

AUNT. The poor man!

DON MARTIN. Every day I arrive at the school trembling,
wondering what they are going to do to me, though, as I
say, they do respect my misfortune. A little while ago
there was a terrible fuss because Mr Consuegra, a
wonderful Latin teacher, found his class register had
been smeared with cat droppings!

AUNT. The little devils!

DON MARTIN. But they pay and we have to put up with
them! Believe me, the parents only laugh at the wicked
pranks they play on us, because we are only assistant
teachers and we don't examine the children. They
think we have no feelings – for them we are people
perched on the lowest rung of the social ladder out of
all those who wear a tie and a starched collar.

AUNT. Ah, Don Martin! What a world we live in!

DON MARTIN. What a world indeed! I always dreamed of
being a poet. I was born with a natural gift and I wrote a
play that was never put on.

AUNT. That would be *Jeptha's Daughter*.

DON MARTIN. Exactly so.

AUNT. Rosita and I have read it. You lent it to us. We've
read it four or five times.

DON MARTIN (*anxiously*). And?

AUNT. I liked it very much. I've always told you that.
Especially when the heroine is about to die and she
remembers her mother and calls out to her.

DON MARTIN. A powerful scene, that one! A true drama.
A play with shape and depth. Impossible to put on the
stage! (*He recites.*)

Oh, mother unequalled! Turn your eyes on
Her who lies before you in wretched trance!

Receive unto yourself these glittering jewels!
Observe the terrible horror of death's advance!

Not at all bad, is it? A fine ring to it, and note the caesura
in 'Observe the terrible horror . . . of death's advance!'

AUNT. Quite wonderful!

DON MARTÍN. And then the part when Glucinius goes to
challenge Isias and looks out from behind the arras.

HOUSEKEEPER (*interrupting him*). Through here!

TWO WORKMEN *enter dressed in overalls.*

FIRST WORKMAN. Afternoon!

AUNT and DON MARTÍN. Good afternoon!

HOUSEKEEPER. This one!

> *She points to a large divan at the back of the room. The men*
> *take it out slowly as if they are removing a coffin. The*
> HOUSEKEEPER *goes out after them. Silence. Two strokes of*
> *a bell are heard as the men take the divan out.*

DON MARTÍN. Is it the novena of St Gertrude the Great?

AUNT. Yes, at St Anthony's.

DON MARTÍN. It's very difficult to be a poet. (*The men*
leave.) After that I wanted to be a chemist. A much
quieter life.

AUNT. My brother – God rest his soul – was a chemist.

DON MARTÍN. But I didn't manage it. I had to help my
mother out, so I became a teacher. That's why I envied
your husband so much. He was what he wanted to be.

AUNT. And it ruined him!

DON MARTÍN. Perhaps, but my situation is worse.

AUNT. But you go on writing.

DON MARTÍN. I don't know why I do it. I've no illusions,
but it's the only thing I like doing. Did you read my
short story? It appeared yesterday in the second issue of
The Intellectual of Granada.

AUNT. You mean *Matilda's Birthday*? Oh yes. We did.
An absolute delight.

DON MARTÍN. You really think so? I wanted to try to be more up-to-date by writing something with a modern atmosphere. I even refer to an aeroplane! Well, you have to keep abreast of things! But still, it's the sonnets I like best of all.

AUNT. To the nine muses of Parnassus!

DON MARTÍN. The ten! The ten! Don't you remember I named Rosita as the tenth muse?

HOUSEKEEPER (*entering*). Madam, help me to fold this sheet. (*The two of them begin to fold it.*) Don Martín with your little red head! Why didn't you marry, you good Christian man? You wouldn't have been so lonely now!

DON MARTÍN. No one ever loved me!

HOUSEKEEPER. Well, there's no good taste left. Why, you've got a lovely way of speaking!

AUNT. You be careful you don't make him fall in love with you!

DON MARTÍN. That'll be the day!

HOUSEKEEPER. When he's got a class in the ground-floor room of the school, I go over to the coalshed to listen: 'What does idea mean?' 'Idea is the intellectual representation of a thing or an object.' Isn't that what you say?

DON MARTÍN. Just listen to her! Listen to her!

HOUSEKEEPER. Yesterday he was bawling out: 'No. This is a hyperbaton', and then 'the epinicion' ... I'd love to be able to understand it, but since I can't always start to laugh. The coalman is always reading a book called *The Ruins of Palmyra*. He looks at me and his eyes are like the glances of two mad cats. But even if I do laugh, because I'm plain ignorant, I know Don Martín's a very clever man.

DON MARTÍN. Nowadays no credit's given to rhetoric and poetry, nor to a university education.

The HOUSEKEEPER *goes out quickly, carrying the folded sheet.*

AUNT. What are we going to do? There's not much time left for us to walk this stage.

DON MARTÍN. We should use it well in acts of kindness and sacrifice.

AUNT. What's that? (*Shouts are heard.*)

HOUSEKEEPER (*entering*). Don Martín! You are wanted at the school! The children have stuck a nail through the water-pipes! All the classrooms are flooded!

DON MARTÍN. I'm going. I dreamt of Parnassus and I have to do the work of a builder or a plumber. As long as they don't push me or I slip . . .

The HOUSEKEEPER *helps* DON MARTÍN *out of his chair.*

HOUSEKEEPER. Alright, alright! . . . Keep calm! Let's hope the water rises so much that not a single child is left!

DON MARTÍN (*leaving*). Praise be to God!

AUNT. Poor man! What a fate!

HOUSEKEEPER. Let him be a mirror to you! He irons his own collars and darns his own socks. When he was ill, I took him some custard, and the sheets on his bed were as black as coal – and the walls, and the washbasin . . . Oh, dear!

AUNT. And other people have so much!

HOUSEKEEPER. That's why I'll always say: 'Damn the rich! Get rid of them all, down to their fingernails!'

AUNT. Let them be!

HOUSEKEEPER. I'm sure they are all going to Hell head-first! Where do you think Don Rafael Salé can be, that exploiter of the poor they buried yesterday! God preserve him – all those priests, all those nuns, all that wailing! In Hell, of course! And he'll be saying: 'I've got twenty million pesetas, don't pinch me with the tongs!

I'll give you two hundred thousand pesetas if you take these hot coals away from my feet!' But those devils – they'll be prodding him here, poking him there, kicking him as hard as they can, smacking him in the face, until his blood is turned to charcoal!

AUNT. All we Christians know that no rich man enters the Kingdom of Heaven, but if you go on talking like that you be careful you don't go to Hell head-first!

HOUSEKEEPER. Me go to Hell? The first push I'll give Old Nick's cauldron will make the hot water reach the edge of the earth. No, madam, no! I'm going to force my way into Heaven. (*Sweetly.*) With you. Each one of us in an armchair of sky-blue silk, rocking herself, fanning ourselves with fans of scarlet satin. And between us, on a swing of jasmine and rosemary sprigs, Rosita, swinging gently, and behind her your husband covered with roses, exactly as he was when he left this room in his coffin; with the same forehead white as crystal. You are rocking yourself like this, and Rosita like this, and behind us our Lord is throwing roses at us, as if the three of us were a float of mother-of-pearl, decorated with candles and flounces in a Holy Week procession.

AUNT. And handkerchiefs to dry our tears will be left down here!

HOUSEKEEPER. And down here they can all manage as best they can! For us up there a time of happiness!

AUNT. Because here every drop has been squeezed from our hearts!

FIRST WORKMAN (*entering*). What would you like done now, madam?

HOUSEKEEPER. Come with me! (*As they go out, she calls back.*) Take heart, madam!

AUNT. God bless you!

She sits down slowly. ROSITA *appears holding a bundle of letters. Silence.*

Have they taken the bureau?

ROSITA. Just a moment ago. Your cousin Esperanza sent a child for a screwdriver.

AUNT. They'll be getting the beds ready for tonight. We should have gone early to do things as we want them. My cousin will have put the furniture any old how.

ROSITA. I'd rather leave when the street is dark. If I could, I'd put the street-lamp out. You can be sure the neighbours will be watching. With the removal-men here, the children have been around the front door all day long, as if someone in the family had died.

AUNT. If I'd only known, I would never have let your uncle mortgage the house with the furniture and everything. We are left with only the barest necessities – a chair to sit on and a bed to sleep in!

ROSITA. Or to die in!

AUNT. What a fine mess he's left us in! Tomorrow the new owners will be here! I wish your uncle could see us! The old fool! No head for business! Off his head with his roses! No concept of money! He was ruining me day by day! 'Oh, Mr So-and-So is here.' And he'd say: 'Show him in'; and he'd come in with empty pockets and go out with them bulging with silver, and always: 'Don't tell my wife!' The prodigal! The coward! And there was no problem he wouldn't try to resolve . . . no children he wouldn't protect, because : . . he had a bigger heart than any man ever had . . . the purest Christian soul . . . Oh, shut up, you old woman! Shut up, you chatterbox, and respect the will of God! We are penniless! Alright! Accept it! But when I see you . . .

ROSITA. Don't worry about me, Aunt! I know the mortgage was to pay for my furniture and my trousseau. That's what really hurts me.

AUNT. He did the right thing. You deserved it all. And everything that was bought is worthy of you and will look a treat the day you use it.

ROSITA. The day I use it?

AUNT. Of course! On your wedding day!

ROSITA. I'd rather not talk about it.

AUNT. That's the trouble with 'decent' women in these parts. Not talking! We don't speak when we should speak. (*Calling out.*) Has the postman come?

ROSITA. What do you intend doing?

AUNT. Letting you see me live, so you can learn from my example!

ROSITA (*embracing her*). Oh, hush!

AUNT. I have to speak out sometime! Get out from these four walls, my child! Don't give in to misfortune!

ROSITA (*kneeling*). I've become accustomed to living outside myself for many years now, thinking about things that were far away . . . And now that these things no longer exist, I find myself going around and around in a cold place, searching for a way out that I'll never find . . . I knew the truth. I knew he'd got married. A kind soul insisted on telling me, but I went on receiving his letters with an illusion full of sadness that surprised even me . . . If no one had said anything; if you hadn't known; if only I had known the truth, his letters and his deceit would have fed my dream as they did in the first year of his absence. But everyone knew the truth and I'd find myself picked out by a pointing finger that ridiculed the modesty of a girl soon to be married and made grotesque the fan of a girl who was still single. Each year that passed was like an intimate piece of clothing torn from my body. One day a friend gets married, and then another, and yet another, and the next day she has a son, and the son grows up and comes to show me his examination marks. Or there are new houses and new songs. And there am I, with the same trembling excitement, cutting the same carnations, looking at the same clouds. And then one day I'm out walking, and I suddenly realise I don't know anyone. Girls and boys leave me behind because I can't keep up, and one of them says: 'There's the old maid'; and another one, a good-looking boy with curly hair says: 'No one's going to fancy her again.' I hear it all and I can't protest against it. I can only go on, with a mouth full of bitterness and a great desire to run away, to take off my shoes, to rest and never move again from my corner.

AUNT. Oh, Rosita, my child!

ROSITA. I'm too old now. Yesterday I heard the housekeeper say that I'd still be able to marry. Never! Don't even think it! I lost that hope when I lost the man I wanted with all my blood, the man I loved . . . and go on loving. Everything's finished . . . and yet, with all my dreams destroyed, I go to bed and get up again with the terrible feeling that hope is finally dead . . . I want to run away, not to be able to see, to be calm, empty . . . Doesn't a poor woman have the right to breathe freely? And yet hope pursues me, circles around me, gnaws at me: like a dying wolf trying to sink his teeth in for the last time.

AUNT. Why didn't you listen to me? Why didn't you marry someone else?

ROSITA. I was tied. And what man ever came to this house sincerely and with a genuine wish to win my affection? No one!

AUNT. You paid no attention to them. You were too dazzled by that lying lover of yours!

ROSITA. Aunt, I've always been serious.

AUNT. You've clung to that one idea with no regard to reality and no thought for your own future.

ROSITA. I am as I am. And I can't change myself. Now the only thing left to me is my dignity. What's here inside me, I keep to myself.

AUNT. That's what I don't want you to do!

HOUSEKEEPER (*coming in suddenly*). Nor me! Speak! Get things off your chest! We'll all have a good cry. We'll all share our feelings.

ROSITA. What can I tell you? There are things that can't be told because there aren't the words to tell them. And even if there were, who would understand their meaning? . . . Oh, you understand if I ask for bread, or water, or even a kiss, but you could never understand nor take away this dark, heavy hand that freezes or burns my heart – I don't know which – whenever I'm alone.

HOUSEKEEPER. At least you've said something!

AUNT. There's consolation for everything!

ROSITA. If I told you the whole story, it would never end. I know my eyes will always be young, but my back will become more bent with every passing day. In any case, what's happened to me has happened to thousands of women. (*Pause.*) But why am I saying all this? (*To the* HOUSEKEEPER.) You, tidy things up! In a few minutes we'll be leaving this house with its garden. And you, Aunt, don't worry about me! (*Pause. To the* HOUSE-KEEPER.) Go on! I don't like you looking at me like that. It annoys me when people have the expression of faithful dogs. (*The* HOUSEKEEPER *leaves.*) Those pitying looks upset me. And they make me angry!

AUNT. Child, what can I do?

ROSITA. Accept things as a lost cause. (*Pause. Walks up and down.*) I know you are thinking about your sister, the old maid . . . an old maid just like me. She was bitter. She hated children and any girl who had a new dress . . . but I won't be like that. (*Pause.*) I'm sorry.

AUNT. Oh, don't be silly!

An eighteen-year-old BOY *appears.*

ROSITA. Come in.

YOUTH. But . . . are you moving?

ROSITA. In a few minutes. When it gets dark.

AUNT. Who is he?

ROSITA. Maria's son.

AUNT. Which Maria?

ROSITA. The oldest of the three Manolas.

AUNT. Oh!

> Those who visit the Alhambra,
> Alone in twos or threes.

You'll have to excuse me, child. My memory's very bad.

YOUTH. You've only seen me a couple of times.

AUNT. I was very fond of your mother. She was a charming person. She died at about the same time as my husband.

ROSITA. It was before that.

YOUTH. Eight years ago now.

ROSITA. He has her face.

YOUTH (*spiritedly*). But not as good as hers. Mine was put together with a hammer!

AUNT. The same sense of humour. Her character.

YOUTH. Of course, I do look like her. At carnival time I put on one of her dresses . . . one she'd had for a long time . . . a green one . . .

ROSITA (*sadly*). With black lace . . . and Nile-green flounces of silk.

YOUTH. Yes.

ROSITA. And a great bow of velvet at the waist.

YOUTH. That's the one.

ROSITA. Falling on either side of the bustle.

YOUTH. What a silly fashion! (*He laughs.*)

ROSITA (*sadly*). But such a pretty fashion.

YOUTH. Oh, don't tell me! There I was, coming downstairs with the dress on, laughing my head off, filling the place with the smell of mothballs, and all of a sudden my aunt started to cry bitterly because she said it was just the same as seeing my mother. Well, it affected me, of course, so I left the dress and the mask on the bed.

ROSITA. There's nothing more alive than a memory. They reach the point where they make our lives impossible. That's why I can well understand those little old women who have taken to drink and wander the streets trying to blot the world out, or sit singing on the seats along the avenue.

AUNT. And how is your married aunt?

YOUTH. She writes to us from Barcelona. Less every time.

ROSITA. Does she have children?

YOUTH. Four.

Pause.

HOUSEKEEPER (*entering*). Give me the keys to the wardrobe.

The AUNT *gives the keys to her. Then, alluding to the* YOUTH.

This boy here was out walking with his sweetheart yesterday. I saw them in the Plaza Nueva. She wanted to walk one way and he wouldn't let her. (*She laughs.*)

AUNT. Let the poor boy be!

YOUTH (*embarrassed*). It was only a joke!

HOUSEKEEPER (*leaving*). Stop blushing then!

ROSITA. Alright, that's enough!

YOUTH. It's a lovely garden you've got.

ROSITA. We used to have!

AUNT. We must cut some flowers.

YOUTH. I hope things turn out well, Doña Rosita.

ROSITA. God be with you, child!

The AUNT *and the* YOUTH *leave. Evening is falling.*

Doña Rosita! Doña Rosita!

She opens in the morning,
And her colour's red and deep.
When evening falls her colour fades,
The whiteness of a salt-stained cheek.
When darkness comes her life ends,
Her soft petals begin to weep.

Pause.

HOUSEKEEPER (*comes in, wearing a shawl*). Time to go!

ROSITA. Yes, I'll get my coat.

HOUSEKEEPER. I've taken the coat-rack down. It's hanging on the window-catch.

The THIRD SPINSTER *enters wearing a dark dress with a mourning veil over her head and a ribbon around her neck in the style of 1912. They speak quietly.*

THIRD SPINSTER. You're off then.

HOUSEKEEPER. In a few minutes.

THIRD SPINSTER. I was giving a piano lesson nearby so I called to see if you needed anything.

HOUSEKEEPER. May God reward you!

THIRD SPINSTER. What a sad state of affairs!

HOUSEKEEPER. Yes, yes. But don't soften my heart! Don't make me weepy! I'm the one who has to bring a bit of life into this mourning without a corpse that you can see here.

THIRD SPINSTER. I'd like to say 'hello' to them.

HOUSEKEEPER. Better not! Call at the other house!

THIRD SPINSTER. Yes. That would be better. But if you need anything! You know I'll do what I can.

HOUSEKEEPER. It's a bad time. But it will pass.

The wind is heard.

THIRD SPINSTER. The wind is rising!

HOUSEKEEPER. Yes. It looks like rain.

The THIRD SPINSTER *leaves.*

AUNT (*entering*). With this wind there won't be a single rose left. The cypresses are almost touching the walls of my room. It's just as if someone wanted to make the garden ugly so that we wouldn't feel sad at leaving it behind.

HOUSEKEEPER. If you mean it was pretty, it was never that! Is your coat done up? Take this scarf. Muffle up! (*Puts it around her.*) Now, when we get there, dinner will be ready. And custard for dessert. Just as you like it. Custard as golden as a marigold!

The HOUSEKEEPER *speaks in a voice choked with emotion. A thud is heard.*

AUNT. That's the greenhouse door! Can't you close it?

HOUSEKEEPER. It won't close. It's swollen with the dampness.

AUNT. It'll be banging all night.

HOUSEKEEPER. Well, we won't hear it . . . !

The stage is in the soft half-light of evening.

AUNT. But I will! I will!

ROSITA *appears. She is pale, dressed in white, with a coat to the hem of her dress.*

HOUSEKEEPER (*courageously*). Let's go!

ROSITA (*in an emotional voice*). It's started to rain. So there won't be anyone at the window watching us leave.

AUNT. Much better if no one sees us.

ROSITA *hesitates, supports herself on a chair and stumbles, to be supported by the* HOUSEKEEPER *and the* AUNT, *who prevent her from falling.*

ROSITA. And when the darkness surrounds her,
Her petals begin to fall.

They leave and the stage is left empty. The door is heard banging. Suddenly a french door at the back blows open and the white curtains flutter in the wind.

Curtain.

Note on the translation of
Doña Rosita the Spinster

Doña Rosita the Spinster differs in several important respects from *Blood Wedding*. Firstly, the characters are mainly middle class, and secondly its mood is, in the first two acts, much more comic. As far as the translation is concerned, the dialogue should suggest, in contrast to *Blood Wedding*, the greater sophistication of the characters, and it is therefore, in general, less stark and austere. In addition, reflecting the comic moments of the play, it is less taut, and there are many instances where the lightness of Lorca's touch and the swift interplay of the characters' exchanges is strongly reminiscent of his earlier farces.

On the other hand, as in Chekhov, this play has perceptible undercurrents of sadness which, by Act Three, rise strongly to the surface. In the dialogue of Rosita and the Aunt, in particular, the mood is once more that of *Blood Wedding* and *Yerma*, and the translation must therefore reflect this movement into a different key.

For the translator the most difficult and challenging aspect of the play is, however, its poetry, which ranges from the deeply touching poem on the rose to the strongly sentimental exchanges between Rosita and her cousin (end of Act One), and the sprightly and largely comic song sung by Rosita and the spinsters in Act Two. In the first and last of the three, Lorca used assonance, in the second a strict rhyme-form. In translating the poetry I have not attempted to follow Lorca in matters of either

155

assonance or rhyme (given the fact that rhymes are easier to find in Spanish), but rather to capture the tone and mood of his extremely beautiful – and sometimes humorous – poems and songs.

Yerma

Translated by Peter Luke

This translation of Yerma *was first presented at the National Theatre, London on 19 March, 1986 with the following cast:*

YERMA	Juliet Stevenson
VICTOR	Neil Budgeon
JUAN	Roger Lloyd-Pack
MARIA	Julia Ford
PAGAN WOMAN	Anne Dyson
FIRST YOUNG GIRL	Shona Morris
SECOND YOUNG GIRL	Katharine Rogers
DOLORES	Heather Tobias
WASHERWOMEN	Celia Imrie
	Christine Absalom
	Shona Morris
	Jenny Galloway
	Katharine Rogers
SISTERS-IN-LAW	Tel Stevens
	Kate Dyson
TOWNSMAN	Richard Bonneville

Directed by	Di Trevis
Designed by	Pamela Howard
	with Bunny Christie
Lighting by	Gerry Jenkinson
Music by	Dominic Muldowney

Act One

Scene One

The curtain rises on a stage lit with a weird dreamlike light. YERMA *is asleep with an embroidery frame at her feet. A* SHEPHERD *enters on tiptoe, leading a small* BOY *dressed in white by the hand. He stares fixedly at* YERMA *for a moment. Then a clock strikes and the* SHEPHERD *goes off. The lighting changes to a sunny morning in springtime.* YERMA *wakes up.*

YERMA (*sings off*).
  For our little baby, baby
  We'll build a hut of straw.
  Out in the fields we'll make it
  And live there evermore.

YERMA. Juan, do you hear me? Juan!

JUAN. Coming.

YERMA. It's time to go.

JUAN. Oxen gone?

YERMA. A while ago.

JUAN. See you later, then.

YERMA. Don't you want this milk?

JUAN. What for?

YERMA. You're too thin with all the work you do.

JUAN. Lean men are like steel.

YERMA. Not you. You were different when we were first married. But look at your face now! It's as if it never saw the light of day. Why don't you go to the river and have a swim? Or go up the roof and let the rain beat down on you. Twenty four months we've been married and you've become sadder and skinnier every day. As if you were growing backwards.

JUAN. Have you done?

YERMA (*getting up*). Don't get me wrong. If I was ill I would like you to take care of me. 'My wife is sick, I'll kill a lamb and make her a good stew. My wife is ill, I'll save this chicken fat to rub on her chest. I'll use the lambskin for her feet when it snows.' That's how I am and that's how I'd take care of you.

JUAN. And I'd be grateful.

YERMA. But you won't let me.

JUAN. There's nothing wrong with me. All these things are in your mind. I work hard, I get older every year and that's all.

YERMA. Every year . . . Just the two of us year after year.

JUAN (*smiling*). And what's wrong with that? The farm's doing well, and no children costing money.

YERMA. No, no children . . . Juan?

JUAN. What?

YERMA. You know I love you?

JUAN. Yes, you love me.

YERMA. I know girls who trembled and cried when they climbed into bed with their husbands. Did I cry the first time I got into bed with you? I sang as I turned back the sheet, didn't I? And I said, 'This linen smells of apples' didn't I?

JUAN. You did.

YERMA. It was my mother who did the crying because I wasn't sorry to leave home. That's the truth. Nobody got married more happily than I did. Only now . . .

JUAN. Shut up. I've got enough work to do without listening to you all day.

YERMA. I know what people are saying. I can see that for myself. Rain loosens stones and makes the mustard grow. People say mustard is no good to anyone. 'Weeds', they say, but rain falls and mustard grows and I like to see the yellow flowers waving in the wind.

JUAN. You must keep hoping.

YERMA. And loving.

> YERMA *rises and takes* JUAN *in her arms, embracing him.*

JUAN. If you want anything just tell me and I'll get it for you. You know I don't like you going out.

YERMA. I never do go out.

JUAN. Good.

YERMA. I suppose so.

JUAN. The street is for people with nothing to do.

YERMA (*resigned*). Of course.

> JUAN *goes out and* YERMA, *turning to her needlework, passes her hand over her belly, raises her arms in a delightful stretch, and settles down to sew.*

YERMA (*singing*).
Where have you come from, my love, my child?
'From the stony mountain cold.'
What do you want, my love, my child?
'That your dress should me enfold.'

> *She threads the needle.*

How the branches dance in the sun
And the fountains splash all about them!

> *As if talking to a child.*

In the patio barks the dog,
And the trees sing in the air.
The oxen low at the herdsman
And the moon puts curls in my hair.
What do you ask of me, child from afar?

> *Pause.*

The white hills of your breast.

How the branches dance in the sun
And the fountains splash all about them!

Sewing.

Hear, little son, for it's true
It's broken I'll be by you
And my poor womb will be torn,
This cradle from which you'll be born.
When, little son, are you going to come?

Pause.

'When your skin smells of jasmine.'

How the branches dance in the sun
And the fountains splash all about them.

As she finishes singing, MARIA *enters with a bundle of clothes.*

YERMA. Maria, where have you come from?
MARIA. The shop.
YERMA. This early?
MARIA. I wanted to be there when they opened. Guess
what I have bought.

YERMA *smiles and shakes her head.*

MARIA. Lace, three reels of thread and some ribbons and
coloured wool! And my husband gave me the money
without a murmur.
YERMA. Are you going to make a new blouse?
MARIA. No! . . . Guess?
YERMA. What?
MARIA. It's . . . Well, it's happened!

YERMA *rises and looks at her in admiration.*

YERMA. After only five months?
MARIA. Yes.
YERMA. Are you sure?

MARIA. Of course.

YERMA. But what do you feel?

MARIA. I don't know ... scared.

YERMA. Scared! (*Taking her in her arms.*) When did you first know? Tell me about it ... Were you a bit careless?

MARIA. I suppose so.

YERMA. What does it feel like?

MARIA. Oh, I don't know. Have you ever held a live bird in your hands?

YERMA. Yes.

MARIA. Well it feels the same – but more inside your blood, somehow.

YERMA. How lovely!

MARIA. It's all so strange. I don't know what to do.

YERMA. What's so strange about it?

MARIA. I don't know what I'm supposed to do. I'd better ask my mother.

YERMA. She's too old now, she'll have forgotten. Don't walk too much and remember when you breathe, breathe as gently as if you held a rose between your teeth.

MARIA. Listen, they say later on you can feel it kicking with its little feet.

YERMA. That's the time you grow to love it even more; when you can start saying: '*my* son,'

MARIA. Sometimes I feel a bit shy.

YERMA. What does your husband say about it?

MARIA. Nothing.

YERMA. Does he love you very much?

MARIA. He never says. But when he comes close to me his eyes tremble like two green leaves.

YERMA. Did he know?

MARIA. Yes.

YERMA. How?

MARIA. I don't know. But on our wedding night he kept

telling me about it over and over with his mouth against my cheek. I feel my baby is a bright bird he slipped into my ear.

YERMA. You're so lucky!

MARIA. But you know more about these things than I do.

YERMA. And much good it's done me!

MARIA. Yes, but why? You're the only one of us left now who . . .

YERMA. I know. But there's still time. Elena took three years. And some older women took longer still. O, but two years and twenty days – it's too long. It's not right that I should be rotting away here. There are nights when I go out onto the patio just to feel the earth under my bare feet. I don't know why. If I go on like this, I'll make myself ill.

MARIA. Ah, come on now, you talk as if you were an old woman already. It's no good moaning. One of my aunts had her first baby after fourteen years, and you should have seen what a lovely little boy he was!

YERMA. What was he like?

MARIA. Rough as a bull, noisy as a cricket. Before he was four months old, he'd pulled our plaits, scratched our faces raw and piddled all over us.

YERMA (*laughing*). But that didn't hurt you.

MARIA. Didn't it just.

YERMA. I have seen my sister feed her child with her breasts covered with scratches. Really painful. But it was a good healthy pain.

MARIA. They say with boys you suffer a lot.

YERMA. That's a lie. Weak women always moan. I don't know why they bother to have children. Of course it's not a bed of roses. I think we lose half our blood. But we have to suffer a bit for the pleasure of watching them grow, and that's good and healthy. It's beautiful. Every woman has blood enough for four or five sons. But if you don't have them your blood turns to poison. That's what's happening to me.

MARIA. I don't know what's happening to me.

YERMA. They always say it's a bit frightening the first time.

MARIA. We'll soon see . . .

YERMA (*taking the bundle of cloth*). Come on, I'll cut you out two little dresses. What's this for?

MARIA. Nappies.

YERMA. Good. (*Sits down.*)

MARIA. Well then, I'll be back soon.

> MARIA *bends to kiss* YERMA, *who runs her hand lovingly over her belly.*

YERMA. Don't run over the cobbles.

MARIA. Goodbye.

> *She kisses her and exits.*

VERMA. Come back soon.

> YERMA *starts to cut material.* VICTOR *enters. He has a strong reassuring presence.*

YERMA. Victor!

VICTOR. Where's Juan?

YERMA. In the fields.

VICTOR. What are you sewing?

YERMA. I am cutting out some nappies.

VICTOR (*smiling*). Good for you.

YERMA (*happily*). I think I might edge them with lace.

VICTOR. If it's a girl you should call her after you.

YERMA. What do you mean?

VICTOR. I'm very happy for you.

YERMA. No . . . They're not for me – they're for Maria's child.

VICTOR. Well, perhaps Maria will set you a good example. This house needs a child.

YERMA. God knows it does.

VICTOR. Then get on with it. Tell your husband there's no point in him sweating his guts out in the fields if there's no one to leave his money to when he's dead. I'm off now with the sheep. Tell Juan he can pick up the two he bought off me when he likes. As for the other – tell him to get going!

He exits smiling.

YERMA (*passionately*). That's it! Get going.

Hear little son, for it's true
It's broken I'll be by you
And my poor womb will be torn,
This cradle from which you'll be born.
When, little son, are you going to come?
When your skin smells of jasmine!

> YERMA *crosses to where* VICTOR *stood. She breathes deeply as if breathing fresh mountain air. Then she crosses to the other side of the room as if looking for something. Finally she returns to her chair, picks up her needlework, and starts to sew but with her thoughts elsewhere.*

Curtain.

Scene Two

A field. YERMA *enters with basket and meets* PAGAN WOMAN.

YERMA. Good day.

PAGAN WOMAN. Good day to you, my lovely. And where are you off to?

YERMA. I've just been taking my husband his food. He's pruning the olives.

PAGAN WOMAN. Been married long?

YERMA. Three years.

PAGAN WOMAN. Kids?

YERMA. No.

PAGAN WOMAN. They'll come soon enough.

YERMA (*hopefully*). You think so?

PAGAN WOMAN. Why not? (*She sits down.*) I've just taken
my old man his dinner. He's old, but he's still working.
He's given me nine boys strong as sunlight but not one
girl, so I have to do all the fetching and carrying myself.

YERMA. Are you from the other side of the river?

PAGAN WOMAN. Yes, by the mill. What family are you?

YERMA. I'm Enrique the Shepherd's daughter.

PAGAN WOMAN. Enrique the Shepherd! I knew him.
Good people. Get up. Sweat. Eat a few loaves of bread
and die. No time for larking about. I could have
married an uncle of yours, but there you are ...
(*Laughs.*) ... I've chucked my skirts over my head in my
time. Oh yes, I've cut myself a good slice of the cake in
my day, I can tell you. Many's the time in the night I've
run to the door thinking I've heard the sound of guitars
at the Fiesta, but it was only the wind. (*Laughs.*) You
may laugh but I've had two husbands and fourteen
sons, five of whom died, and yet I'm not sad and I'd like
to live a good while longer yet. But it's like I always say,
look at the fig trees how long they last! And the houses!
It's only us blessed women who go to rot.

YERMA. I want to ask you a question.

PAGAN WOMAN. Let me look at you ... Yes, I know what
you're going to ask and it's something I can't answer.
(*She gets up.*)

YERMA (*restrains her*). Why not? You've given me heart.
I've needed to talk to someone older. There's something I need to know ... something you can tell me.

PAGAN WOMAN. What?

YERMA (*dropping her voice*). What you know. Why am I childless? Must I spend the rest of my life feeding chickens and hanging neat little curtains in the windows? Tell me what to do and I'll do it even if I have to stick pins in my eyeballs.

PAGAN WOMAN. Me? What can I tell you? I just lay flat on my back, started to sing and kids came like water. You've got a lovely body. Why don't you do something about it? There are plenty of stallions kicking at the stable door. Now leave me alone, my girl, and don't start me talking, or I'll say something I shouldn't.

YERMA. But why? This is all we talk about, my husband and I.

PAGAN WOMAN. Listen, do you like it with your husband?

YERMA. What do you mean?

PAGAN WOMAN. Do you love him? Do you long for him?

YERMA. I don't know.

PAGAN WOMAN. Don't you tremble when he comes near you? When he touches you with his lips don't you go weak all over? Well, come on! Don't you?

YERMA. No, I have never felt like that, never.

PAGAN WOMAN. Never? Not even dancing?

YERMA. Well, yes, once – with Victor.

PAGAN WOMAN. Go on.

YERMA. He held me once around the waist. I couldn't speak. I couldn't breathe. And another time I was only fourteen, Victor – he was a big strong lad – took me in his arms to jump a ditch and I shook so much my teeth were chattering. But then I was shy.

PAGAN WOMAN. What about your husband?

YERMA. My husband. That's different. My father found him for me and I took him. Happily. And that's the honest truth. Then from the moment we were engaged I had no other thought but – children. When I looked at him, I could see myself reflected in his eyes, very small, very docile, as if I were my own child.

PAGAN WOMAN. Perhaps that's why you haven't got kids yet. Me I was just the opposite. Men like to pleasure us, girl. They like to undo our plaits and give us water to drink from their own mouths. That's what makes the world go round.

YERMA. Yours perhaps; not mine. It's my mind goes round and round and all I feel and all I think about is where is my son? When I give myself to my husband it's just for that. Not for pleasure – never for pleasure.

PAGAN WOMAN (*Patting* YERMA*'s stomach*). No wonder that's still empty.

YERMA. But I'm not empty. I'm filling up with hate. Is it my fault? Is it just for men, bed? What am I supposed to think lying there on my back staring at the ceiling while he turns over and goes to sleep? Him or that sweet child that will come one day and be held shining at my breast? I don't know. But if you know, then tell me for God's sake. (*She drops on her knees.*)

PAGAN WOMAN. Oh, what a peach! Oh, what a lovely innocent creature you are! Only leave off now and don't keep me talking any more. You've got your pride and I don't want to meddle with anyone's pride. You've got a mind of your own, only just don't be so innocent, that's all.

YERMA (*sadly*). Everything's kept such a secret for girls like me, brought up in the country. All hints and half-truths. Things are never talked about. And you're as bad as the rest of them. You're like a doctor. You know what it's all about. Here I am dying of thirst and you won't give me a drop of water.

PAGAN WOMAN. I'd tell a calmer woman. Not you, though. I'm an old woman and I know what I know.

YERMA. Then God help me.

PAGAN WOMAN. God! Never mind God. I've never

thought much of him anyway. Men are more likely to help you than God.

YERMA. Why? Why do you say that? Why?

PAGAN WOMAN (*leaving*). There ought to be a God, if only a little one, to strike down with lightning those men whose bad blood blights the earth.

YERMA. I don't know what you're talking about.

PAGAN WOMAN. But I do know what I'm talking about. It's not the end of the world; look on the bright side. You're still young. What more can I say?

PAGAN WOMAN *exits. Two* YOUNG GIRLS *come in.*

FIRST GIRL. Hullo. We keep running into people wherever we go. What's going on?

YERMA. The usual: the men prune the olives, the women feed the men, and the old people stay at home. What else?

SECOND GIRL. Going back to the village?

YERMA. Yes.

FIRST GIRL. I must get a move on. I left the baby asleep and there's no one at home.

YERMA. Then go! You must never leave babies. Supposing the pigs got into the house.

FIRST GIRL. You're right. I'd better hurry.

YERMA. Go on, then. That's how accidents happen. I suppose you locked him in.

FIRST GIRL. Of course.

YERMA. You forget how helpless a child is. So many things can happen. They can swallow buttons or prick themselves with a needle – anything.

FIRST GIRL. I must run. I just never think about these things.

YERMA. Run! Hurry!

FIRST GIRL *exits.*

SECOND GIRL. If you had four or five kids about the

house you wouldn't be so fussy.

YERMA. I would – however many I had.

SECOND GIRL. But you haven't, any more than I have. So life's nice and peaceful.

YERMA. Peaceful? Not for me.

SECOND GIRL. For me it is. The only trouble is my mother never stops stuffing me with herbs and that to try and make me pregnant. And then when October comes round she drags me off to that old Saint who's supposed to give you babies if you pray hard enough. Well, she can pray as much as she likes but you won't catch me.

YERMA. Why did you get married then?

SECOND GIRL. Get married? Doesn't everyone? My parents wanted me out of the house. The way it's going the only ones left single will be the under-twelves. Anyway, we were really married long before we got to the Church. It's the old people who push you into those sort of things. I'm nineteen, I hate housework and if you're always doing the things you hate what's the point of life? Is my husband any better to me now than he was before? We still do the same sort of things, don't we? Marriage is old-fashioned rubbish.

YERMA. Shut up. Don't talk like that.

SECOND GIRL. You think I'm barmy; the barmy girl! The crazy girl! (*Laughs.*) But the one thing life has taught me is that most people spend their lives bottled up inside their houses doing the things they hate. But I like dressing up and feeling everybody's eyes on me when I walk down the street. I please myself. I'd swim naked in the stream and ring the Church bells if I felt like it; and when I'm in the mood I'll take a drink with any man.

YERMA. You're just a kid.

SECOND GIRL. Maybe, but I'm not stupid! (*She laughs.*)

YERMA. Is that your mother that lives at the top of

the village?

SECOND GIRL. Yes.

YERMA. The last house?

SECOND GIRL. Yes.

YERMA. What's her name?

SECOND GIRL. Dolores. Why?

YERMA. Nothing.

SECOND GIRL. Are you asking because . . . ?

YERMA. I don't know. I just wondered.

SECOND GIRL. Did you now! Well, I must go and feed my old man, I suppose. Pity I can't still call him my boyfriend. Ah, well, that barmy girl is off. Bye.

 SECOND GIRL *exits laughing happily.*

YERMA. 'Bye.

 VICTOR *is heard singing off.*

VICTOR (*off*). Why do you sleep alone, shepherd?
Why do you sleep alone?
On my blanket of wool
You'd sleep softly, shepherd,
Why do you sleep alone?

 YERMA *is listening.*

Why do you sleep alone, shepherd?
Why do you sleep alone?
In my woollen bed
You'd lie warmer, shepherd,
Than in your croft of gloomy stone.
In your frosty shirt
Last winter's reeds
Make draughty bedding, shepherd,
The holm-oak a spiky pillow.
And if you hear a woman's voice, shepherd,
It is but the voice of broken water.

Shepherd, shepherd,

What does the mountain want of you.
That mountainside of bitter herbs?
What child is killing you?
The hard thorns of the furze!

YERMA *starts to go out but stumbles into* VICTOR *as he enters.*

VICTOR. Where does this pretty girl think she's going?

YERMA. Was that you singing?

VICTOR. It was.

YERMA. I've never heard you sing before.

VICTOR. No?

YERMA. That's quite a voice – it flows out of your mouth like a fountain.

VICTOR. Because I'm feeling happy today.

YERMA. So I see.

VICTOR. More than I can say for you.

YERMA. I'm not really sad, though I have reason to be.

VICTOR. At least you're not like your husband.

YERMA. You mean, dried up?

VICTOR. He always was. Where've you been? Taking him his dinner?

YERMA. Yes. (*She looks at him.*) What've you got there? (*She points at his face.*)

VICTOR. Where?

She comes close to him.

VICTOR. Oh, it's nothing.

YERMA. It looks to me like –

VICTOR. A scratch I expect.

YERMA. Perhaps.

They stand motionless in silence. The tension between them is acute.

YERMA. Listen!

VICTOR. What?

YERMA. Can't you hear crying?

VICTOR (*listening*). No.

YERMA. I thought I heard a child crying.

VICTOR. What?

YERMA. Very close. As if it was drowning.

VICTOR. There's always a lot of kids round here, come to pinch the fruit.

YERMA. But it was a baby's voice.

VICTOR. I can't hear anything.

YERMA. I must have imagined it.

She gazes at him intently. He holds her gaze, then looks away as if afraid. JUAN *enters.*

JUAN. What are you doing here still?

YERMA. Talking.

VICTOR. Well. I'm off. (*Exits.*)

JUAN. You should have been back home by now.

YERMA. I was enjoying myself.

JUAN. What's been keeping you?

YERMA. It was a lovely day and the birds were singing.

JUAN. That's all very well but it's just the way to start people talking.

YERMA (*fiercely*). What are you trying to say? What are you hinting at, Juan?

JUAN. I'm not saying it's you. It's other people.

YERMA. Well they can fuck themselves.

JUAN. Don't swear. It doesn't suit a woman.

YERMA. If only I was a woman – a real woman.

JUAN. Don't start. Why don't you go home?

YERMA. All right. Shall I wait up for you?

JUAN. No. I've got to irrigate the fruit trees all night. The water is low and I've only got it till sun-up. If I don't watch out the others will switch it. You go to bed and get some sleep.

YERMA. Sleep! Oh yes I'll sleep!

She exits.

Curtain.

Act Two

Scene One

A fast flowing mountain stream where the village women, at different levels, are washing their clothes. As the curtain rises they are singing.

WASHERWOMEN (*singing*). I'll wash your ribbons
In the cold, cold stream.
And laugh with the laughter
Of the warm jasmine.

FIRST WOMAN. Gossip.

SECOND WOMAN. Everyone gossips here.

FOURTH WOMAN. There's no harm in it.

FIFTH WOMAN. Those who look for respect, let them earn it.

FOURTH WOMAN. Those who live in glass houses shouldn't throw stones.

Laughter.

FIFTH WOMAN. You said it.

FIRST WOMAN. The trouble is you never get the true story.

FOURTH WOMAN. All the same, facts are facts. The husband has had to bring his two sisters in to live with them.

FIFTH WOMAN. Those two old crows?

FOURTH WOMAN. Yes. They used to keep an eye on the Church. Now they're keeping an eye on the sister-in-law. You wouldn't catch me living with that pair.

FIRST WOMAN. Why not?

FOURTH WOMAN. They give me the creeps. They're like weeds in a graveyard. And I'll bet they eat candle-grease and cook it in lamp-oil.

THIRD WOMAN. Have they moved in yet?

FOURTH WOMAN. Yesterday. Now he can get out again to the fields.

FIRST WOMAN. What's supposed to have happened, then?

FIFTH WOMAN. Well, you know how cold it was the other night. She spent the whole night sitting out on the doorstep.

FIRST WOMAN. Whatever for?

FOURTH WOMAN. She can't stand it indoors.

FIFTH WOMAN. Some women get like that if they haven't had kids – larking about on rooftops or paddling in rivers.

FIRST WOMAN. Who are you to talk? It's not her fault she hasn't got kids.

FOURTH WOMAN. Those that want them get them. But some of these girls today just don't want to get a wrinkled belly.

They laugh.

THIRD WOMAN. Nowadays it's all painted faces, carnations in the hair and other women's men.

FIFTH WOMAN. That's the truth and no mistake.

FIRST WOMAN. But has anyone ever seen her with another man?

FOURTH WOMAN. Not me, but they say she's been seen.

FIRST WOMAN. They say . . . Who says?

FIFTH WOMAN. They say twice at least –

SECOND WOMAN. What were they doing?

FOURTH WOMAN. Talking.

FIRST WOMAN. Talking's no sin.

FOURTH WOMAN. No, but it was the looks. As my mother used to say, there's ways and ways of looking. No woman looks at a rosebush the same way as she looks at the bulge in a man's trousers – and she wasn't looking at no rosebush.

FIRST WOMAN. Who was it then?

FOURTH WOMAN. Oh, a certain someone. Do you want me to spell it out? If you haven't heard you can find out for yourself. And you can take it from me out of sight doesn't mean out of mind.

FIRST WOMAN. That's a lie!

Excited reactions.

FIFTH WOMAN. And what about him?

THIRD WOMAN. Oh, he's as dozy as a lizard in the sun.

Laughter.

FIRST WOMAN. She'd be right as rain if they had kids.

SECOND WOMAN. The trouble with some people is they don't know when they're well off.

FOURTH WOMAN. That house must be a living hell what with her and the in-laws never speaking a word and the whole place scrubbed, whitewashed and waxed from floor to ceiling even when it doesn't need it. The better it looks outside the worse it gets inside.

FIRST WOMAN. He's the one to blame. If a man can't do right by his wife then he'd best look out.

FOURTH WOMAN. She's the one to blame with that nagging tongue of hers.

FIRST WOMAN. What in buggeration's got into you lot talking like that?

FOURTH WOMAN. And who asked you to speak?

SECOND WOMAN. Shut your bloody gob.

FIRST WOMAN. And I'd like to stitch your tongues up.

FOURTH WOMAN. And flatten those false tits of yours.

SECOND WOMAN. Shut up, the two of you! There's the two coming now.

There is whispering as YERMA's *two* SISTERS-IN-LAW

*arrive, both dressed in black There is a long silence as they start
to do their washing. Sound of sheep bells off.*

FIRST WOMAN. Look! There go the shepherds.

THIRD WOMAN. That's right, all the flocks are going up to
the mountains.

FOURTH WOMAN. I love the smell of sheep.

THIRD WOMAN. Do you?

FOURTH WOMAN. And why not? It's natural. And
I like the smell of the red silt washed down by the river
in winter.

THIRD WOMAN. No accounting for taste.

FIFTH WOMAN. Look, all the flocks leaving together.

FOURTH WOMAN. It's like a flood of wool. If that young
corn had eyes to see it would be trembling now all right.

THIRD WOMAN. Just look at them run.

FIRST WOMAN. There. That's the whole lot now, isn't it?

FOURTH WOMAN. Let's see, yes. No. No, there's still
some to come.

FIFTH WOMAN. Whose?

FOURTH WOMAN. Victor's.

> *The two* SISTERS-IN-LAW *straighten up and look at each
> other. The* WOMEN *pick up their song.*

FOURTH WOMAN. I'll wash your ribbons
In the cold, cold stream.
And laugh with the laughter
Of warm jasmine.
I want to live
In a little snow-fall of jasmine.

FIRST WOMAN. Alas, for the barren wife!
Alas, for her sand-filled breasts!

FIFTH WOMAN. Tell me does your husband
Give you such a thing
That when you wash your petticoat
It makes the water sing.

FOURTH WOMAN. Your shirt is a ship of silver
With the white wind in its sails.

FIRST WOMAN. I'm going to wash my baby's clothes
To teach the stream a lesson,
How to be as bright as glass,
And stay as clear as crystal.

SECOND WOMAN. From the mountain my husband
Came home for his tea.
He brought me a rose
And I gave him three.

FIFTH WOMAN. From the valley my husband
Came home to dine.
He brought me sweet myrtle
And I gave him wine.

FOURTH WOMAN. On the wind came my husband
Back home to his bed.
I gave him red wallflowers,
Wallflowers red.

FIRST WOMAN. Flower with fallen flower lies
As the reaper's blood in summer dries.

SECOND WOMAN. And thighs must open to he who wakes
When winter wind the door-jamb shakes.

FIRST WOMAN. And the bed-sheets must be made
to groan –

FOURTH WOMAN. And to sing!

FIFTH WOMAN. When the man comes
To claim his own.

FOURTH WOMAN. Because our arms are locked together.

SECOND WOMAN. Because light catches in our throats.

FOURTH WOMAN. Because we are entered by the thrust-
ing branch.

FIRST WOMAN. And covered by the mountain wind.

SIXTH WOMAN (*appearing at the top of the waterfall*).
So that a child can raise
High windows to the dawn.

FIRST WOMAN. And our body is torn by angry branches
of coral.

SIXTH WOMAN. So that there may be oarsmen to row
on the sea.

FIRST WOMAN. A boy, a little boy.

SECOND WOMAN. And the doves spread their wings and
open their beaks.

THIRD WOMAN. And a little boy cries. My son.

FOURTH WOMAN. And the men stumble forward like
wounded stags.

FIFTH WOMAN. O, the joy, the joy, the joy,
Of a round belly beneath one's petticoat.

SECOND WOMAN. O, the joy, the joy, the joy,
Of a navel, that sweet and tender cup.

FIRST WOMAN. But alas for the barren wife!
Alas for her whose breasts are filled with sand!

THIRD WOMAN. How she shines!

SECOND WOMAN. How she runs!

FIFTH WOMAN. How she shines again!

FIRST WOMAN. How she sings!

SECOND WOMAN. How she hides!

FIRST WOMAN. And how she sings again!

SIXTH WOMAN. O, the day that my little boy first lay
in my lap.

SECOND WOMAN. I'll wash your ribbons
In the cold, cold stream.
And laugh with the laughter
Of warm jasmine.
Ha! ha! ha!

They wash and beat the clothes to the rhythm of the song.

Curtain.

Scene Two

YERMA*'s house – evening.* JUAN *is seated. His two* SISTERS *are standing.*

JUAN. You say she's just gone out?

The elder SISTER *nods.*

I suppose she's at the fountain, but you know I don't like her going out by herself . . . You might as well lay the table. (*They start to do so.*) A man is what he eats. I was at it all day yesterday pruning the apples and by the time I'd done I asked myself why I sweat my guts out if I haven't strength left to raise hand to mouth. I'm sick of this . . . Where's she gone? One of you ought to have gone out with her. That's what you're here for – not just sitting at my table and drinking my wine. My work may be out in the fields, but my good name is here at home. And my name is your name so you needn't pull long faces.

YERMA *comes in and stands at the door carrying two pitchers of water.*

Where have you been – at the fountain?

YERMA. You want fresh water don't you? How's the work going?

The SISTERS *go out.*

JUAN. I was pruning all yesterday.

YERMA *sets the pitchers down.*

YERMA. Are you finished for the day?

JUAN. I've got to see about the sheep and I'm the only one can do that.

YERMA. So you keep saying.

JUAN. A man has his job to do.

YERMA. And a woman should have too. I'm not asking you to stay. Your two watchdogs'll keep a good eye on me. Anyway the bread is baked, the cheese is made and the mutton is stewing in its own juice – and so am I. You should be feeling all right, your sheep on the mountain and the pasture wet with dew.

JUAN. A man needs peace of mind.

YERMA. And you don't have that?

JUAN. No, I do not.

YERMA. Don't start.

JUAN. You go out too much. I've said it before. The place for the sheep is the sheep-fold and the place for the woman is the home.

YERMA. All right. In the home – but not buried alive. Home should be a place where the chairs are broken and the bed-linen worn out with use. But here, no. When I get into my bed at night it's as bright and shiny as the day it was bought.

JUAN. There you are, you see. No wonder I have to keep an eye on you.

YERMA. What for? What have I done? I've always been a dutiful wife and if my life's not all I'd hoped for, at least I keep it to myself, so let's say no more about it. I'll learn to live with it. Don't ask any more of me that's all. If I was suddenly turned into an old woman with a mouth like a shrivelled quince, you'd be happy I suppose. Oh well, it's my cross and I've got to bear it, so leave me alone.

JUAN. I just don't understand you. I begrudge you nothing. If there's anything special you want I send to the village for it. I know I've got my faults but all I want is a quiet life and when I have to sleep out in the fields I want to feel that you are here sleeping peacefully in the house.

YERMA. But I don't sleep. How can I sleep?

JUAN. Then for God's sake what do you want? Tell me! Tell me!

YERMA (*looking at him very deliberately*). You know what I want.

Pause.

JUAN. The same old story, eh? It's five years now, isn't it. I'd almost got over it.

YERMA. You might – not me. It's different for you men: pruning trees, price of sheep, market day. But all we women have got is babies and bringing up of children. Without that we're nothing.

JUAN. Each to his own. Everybody's made differently. Get one of your brother's children over here. Why not? I wouldn't mind.

YERMA. Someone else's child? My arms would turn to ice.

JUAN. You're just driving yourself mad with all this. Banging your head against a wall.

YERMA. It's not natural that there should be a wall here at all. There should be flowers and fresh spring water.

JUAN. Why can't you just shut up and accept things as they are?

YERMA. Accept things? D'you think I came to this house just to accept things? When they put me in my coffin with a rag tied under my chin and my hands joined together, then I'll accept things. But not before.

JUAN. So what do you want to do about it?

YERMA. I'm thirsty but there is neither glass nor water. I want to climb mountains but I have no feet. I need to sew my petticoat but I can find neither needle nor thread.

JUAN. You're not a normal woman. You just want to destroy yourself and drag me down with you.

YERMA. I don't know what's the matter with me. I only know that I've never done you any wrong, never. So just leave me alone and I'll get over it on my own.

JUAN. I just don't want fingers pointing at me in the street.

So from now on this door stays shut and you stay behind it.

One of the SISTERS *comes in and goes slowly to the cupboard.*

YERMA. It's not a sin to talk to people, is it?
JUAN. That depends.

The other SISTER *comes in and fills a jug from a pitcher.*

JUAN (*lowering his tone*). I've had enough. If anybody speaks to you just keep your mouth shut and remember you're a married woman.
YERMA. A married woman!
JUAN. And remember that this family has its self-respect and that reflects on every one of us.

The SISTER *with the jug goes slowly out.*

this self-respect runs deep, but can easily be destroyed.

The other SISTER *follows with a dish in procession. Pause.*

I'm sorry. We'll say no more.

YERMA *looks at her husband. He raises his eyes to her gaze.*

Why am I sorry? I should put you under lock and key.

The two SISTERS *appear in the doorway.*

YERMA. I've got nothing more to say.
JUAN. Let's eat.

The SISTERS *go out.*

D'you hear me?
YERMA (*quietly*). Eat with your sisters. I'm not hungry.
JUAN. Just as you like. (*He follows his* SISTERS.)
YERMA (*As in a dream*).
  O, field of sorrow!
  O, door locked to loveliness!
  That I must beg to bear a son
  When the wind offers
  Only dahlias of the sleeping moon.

Dahlias of the sleeping moon . . .
These two breasts of mine
That should now fill with warm milk
Are two hard pulses
Throbbing in my flesh,
Shaking the branches of my bitterness.
O, blind breasts beneath my dress!
O, blank-eyed doves!
O, pain of imprisoned blood,
That pricks my belly
As though it were swarmed by wasps!
But you must come, my love, my child.
Because the sea gives salt, and the earth fruit.
And because the womb holds tender sons
The way soft clouds hold rain.

She looks out of the door.

Maria, why do you rush past like that?

MARIA *comes in with her baby.*

MARIA. Because I've got the baby with me. It always seems to make you cry.

YERMA. I know. (*Takes the baby and sits down.*)

MARIA. I hate to make you envious. It makes me sad.

YERMA. It isn't envy, it's despair.

MARIA. You mustn't say that.

YERMA. How can I help it when I see you and all the others in full bloom while I'm withering away.

MARIA. You'd be much happier if only you'd listen to me. You've got so many other things.

YERMA. A childless woman is like a bunch of thistles – something fit for God's rubbish heap.

MARIA *goes as if to take the child.*

Take him. He'll be happier with you. I've no right even to pretend I'm a mother.

MARIA. How can you say that?

YERMA (*she gets up*). Because I'm sick and weary. Weary of being a woman not put to proper use. I'm hurt, hurt and humbled beyond endurance watching the crops springing up, the fountains flowing, the ewes bearing lambs and bitches their litter of pups, until it seems the whole countryside is teeming with mothers nursing their sleeping young. And here am I with two hammers beating at my breasts where my baby's mouth should be.

MARIA. I hate to hear you talk like that.

YERMA. You mothers have no idea what it is like for us, any more than a swimmer in a mountain stream ever thinks of what it's like to be dying of thirst.

MARIA. Must I say it all over again –

YERMA. The greater my need, the less hope there seems to be.

MARIA. That's a terrible thing to say.

YERMA. I will end up thinking I'm turning into my own son. Some nights I even go down to feed the oxen – and no woman ever does that – and then as I walk through the barn in the darkness I seem to hear my own footsteps and they sound like the footsteps of a man.

MARIA. Everybody has some purpose in life.

YERMA. Yet all my longing persists. So now you see what my life is!

MARIA. What about the sisters-in-law?

YERMA. You'll see me dead in a ditch before I ever speak to either of them.

MARIA. And your husband?

YERMA. It's three against one.

MARIA. What do they do?

YERMA. They invent things to salve their consciences. They try to make out I'm thinking about another man. They haven't the sense to know that even if I was, my pride would never let me do anything about it. Men don't mean a thing to me. But what they don't seem to realise is if I wanted to I could destroy the whole family forever.

One of the SISTERS *appears and goes out with a loaf of bread.*

MARIA. But I'm sure your husband loves you still.

YERMA. My husband gives me bread and a roof.

MARIA. Oh it's all terrible! But you must think of Our Lord and what he had to suffer.

They reach the door.

YERMA (*looking at the baby*). Look, he's awake.

MARIA. He'll start singing in a minute.

YERMA. He's got your eyes. Did you know that? They're your eyes, don't you see? He's got exactly the same eyes as you.

YERMA *starts to cry and pushes* MARIA *gently out. She is about to go inside the house again when she is stopped by the* SECOND GIRL.

SECOND GIRL. Psst!

YERMA. What is it?

SECOND GIRL. I was waiting till she left. My mother's expecting you.

YERMA. Is she alone?

SECOND GIRL. With two of the neighbours.

YERMA. Will you ask her to wait.

SECOND GIRL. You're really going then? You're not scared?

YERMA. I'm going.

SECOND GIRL. That's up to you.

YERMA. Ask them to wait if I'm late.

VICTOR *comes in.*

VICTOR. Is Juan in?

YERMA. Yes.

SECOND GIRL (*covering up*). I'll bring the blouse round later then.

YERMA. All right.

GIRL *goes.*

(*To* VICTOR.) Sit down.

VICTOR. No, I'm fine.

YERMA (*calling*). Juan!

VICTOR. I've come to say goodbye.

He is trembling slightly, but tries to appear calm.

YERMA. You off to join your brothers, then?

VICTOR. That's what my father wants.

YERMA. He must be getting on now.

VICTOR. Yes, he's getting on.

YERMA. Well, it'll make a change.

VICTOR. One field of sheep looks much like another.

YERMA. Not to me. I'd like to go far away!

VICTOR. What's the difference? Same sheep, same wool.

YERMA. For men, maybe. But it's different for women. I've yet to hear a man sit down to a meal and say how good the apples were. You take what's put in front of you without a word of complaint. But as for me, I'm sick of the very water in these wells.

VICTOR. Maybe so.

The stage is in soft shadow.

YERMA. Victor?

VICTOR. What?

YERMA. Why are you really going? Everybody round here likes you.

VICTOR. I've tried to keep my nose clean.

YERMA. Oh, yes, you've always behaved yourself. But I remember a shepherd-boy who once held me in his arms. Don't you remember? Don't you know what happened?

VICTOR. Things change.

YERMA. Some things never change. Things that happen behind walls and locked doors cannot change because nobody ever hears about them.

VICTOR. That's the way of it.

The second SISTER *appears and makes her way to the doorway where she stands silhouetted against the sunset.*

YERMA. But if ever these walls were broken down, all hell would break loose.

VICTOR. What would be the good? The stream would still flow at the bottom of the orchard, the sheep would stay in the fold, the moon in the sky and the man behind his plough. You can't change things.

YERMA. It's hard not to have the wisdom of the old.

The long and melancholy call of the shepherd's horn is heard in the distance.

VICTOR. There go the sheep.

JUAN *enters.*

JUAN. You off now?

VICTOR. I want to get to the pass before daybreak.

JUAN. No complaints about our deal?

VICTOR. No, you always paid a fair price.

JUAN (*to* YERMA). I bought his ewes off him.

YERMA. Did you?

VICTOR (*to* YERMA). Yes, they're yours now.

YERMA. I didn't know.

JUAN (*pleased*). We shook hands on it.

VICTOR. Juan's land will overflow.

YERMA. He who has sheep, has fleeces.

The SISTER *who has been standing by the door now comes in.*

JUAN. We've hardly got room for them now.

YERMA (*gloomily*). It's a wide world.

Pause.

JUAN (to VICTOR). I'll go with you as far as the river.

VICTOR (*shaking* YERMA *by the hand*). Good luck to this house.

YERMA. Please God! . . . Good luck!

VICTOR *is about to go but turns suddenly.*

VICTOR. What did you say?

YERMA. I said, Good luck.

VICTOR. Thanks.

JUAN *and* VICTOR *go.* YERMA *stands for a moment looking at the hand she gave* VICTOR. *She moves quickly to pick up a shawl.*

SECOND GIRL (*appearing silently, her head covered in a shawl*). Let's go.

YERMA. Yes. Let's go.

They go out furtively. Darkness has nearly fallen. The first SISTER *appears with an oil-lamp which should be the only source of light on the stage. She moves downstage looking for* YERMA. *The sound of a shepherd's horn sounds off.*

FIRST SISTER (*in a low voice*). Yerma!

The shepherd's horns are heard again. The second SISTER *now appears. They glance at each other and make their way to the door.*

SECOND SISTER (*louder*). Yerma!

FIRST SISTER (*going to the door and shouting*). Yerma!

Distant shepherd's horns are heard and sheep bells. The stage is in total darkness.

Curtain.

Act Three

Scene One

The house of DOLORES, *the wise-woman. Almost daybreak. Enter* YERMA *with* DOLORES *and two* OLD WOMEN.

DOLORES. You've got guts, I'll say that for you.

FIRST OLD WOMAN. If you want something badly enough you'll do anything.

SECOND OLD WOMAN. It was certainly dark enough in the cemetery.

DOLORES. Many's the time I've held prayers in the cemetery with women wanting a child and they were all scared stiff – except you.

YERMA. I've come for results. I know you're not a fake.

DOLORES. And so you should. May I drop dead and my mouth be filled with ants if I ever told a lie. The last one to come to me was an old beggar-woman who had been barren far longer than you. But her belly ripened so sweetly she had twins down there by the river before she ever had time to reach the village. She brought them back to me herself in a cloth for me to wash.

YERMA. She walked by herself from the river?

DOLORES. By herself. Her shoes and skirt soaked in blood – but her face was shining.

YERMA. Was she all right?

DOLORES. Why shouldn't she be? If it's God's will.

YERMA. Yes, if it's God's will nothing could go wrong. To pick up your babies and wash them in running water! Animals lick their new-born, don't they? I wouldn't mind what I did for my child. I want to feel this great glow inside as the tiny creature sleeps against me, to listen to the warm stream of milk filling my breasts till it's so full it turns its milky mouth away. 'Come on, one more, baby, one more little suck.' To see the drops of milk spill down its little chin.

DOLORES. You'll have your baby. You can count on it.

YERMA. I'll have it because I've got to have it, or there's no sense in the world. But sometimes when I feel sure that I never, never will – I feel a white-hot ball of flame rising up from my feet and burning my belly. And then men in the street, bulls in the field and even stones in the road seem to be made of cotton wool. And it's then I ask myself what in the name of God is life.

FIRST OLD WOMAN. It's natural for a woman to want kids, but if she doesn't get them, why worry? Take life as you find it. Don't find fault with it. I know I went along with the prayers and all that, but when all's said and done what would be the future for a kid of yours? He wouldn't be born with a silver spoon in his mouth, would he?

YERMA. I'm not thinking of the future. I'm thinking of today. You're old and you see life as a book that you know by heart. But I'm desperate for what should be mine by rights. I want to hold my son in my arms and sleep in peace. Listen – and don't think I'm mad, but even if I knew my child would grow up to hate me and drag me through the streets by the hair, I would still bless the day he was born. It's better to weep for a life that destroys me than this poison that year after year lies buried in my heart.

FIRST OLD WOMAN. You young people, you never listen to advice. But while you're waiting for God's grace, why not take comfort in the love of your husband?

YERMA. A lot of comfort there is there!

DOLORES. He's a good man.

YERMA. Oh yes, he's a good man all right. I wouldn't care if he beat me. But no. He works in the fields all day and when he comes home at night he sits down and counts his money. When he makes love to me, it is a duty. Cold as a corpse. I have always hated women who brag about their sexiness, but there are times now when I'm on fire – a fire no water can quench.

DOLORES. Yerma!

YERMA. No, I'm not a whore, but I know a child's born of man and woman. Oh, if only I could have one by myself!

DOLORES. Don't you think your husband suffers too?

YERMA. He does not suffer. He doesn't want children.

FIRST OLD WOMAN. How can you say that?

YERMA. D'you think I don't know him? If he wanted them he'd give them to me wouldn't he? I don't love him. I don't love him, but he's all I've got. I am honour bound to him. He's my only hope.

FIRST OLD WOMAN (*anxiously*). It's beginning to get light. You'd better get home.

DOLORES. The men will soon be out with the cattle. It wouldn't do for you to be seen out alone.

YERMA. It's been a relief to talk. How often am I supposed to say these prayers?

DOLORES. The Laurel prayer twice a day and the prayer to St Anne at noon. And when you know you're pregnant, you can bring me the two bushels of wheat you promised me.

FIRST OLD WOMAN. I can see daylight on the hilltops. Go now.

DOLORES. Go round by the water-course before people start opening their doors.

YERMA (*despairing*). Oh God, why did I come?

DOLORES. Are you regretting it?

YERMA. No.

DOLORES. I'll come with you as far as the corner, if
you're scared.

FIRST OLD WOMAN. It'll be broad daylight before
you get home.

Voices are heard.

DOLORES. Quiet!

They all listen.

FIRST OLD WOMAN. It's nobody. Go with God.

As YERMA *makes her way to the door, loud knocking is heard.*

DOLORES. Who's there?

VOICE. It's me.

YERMA. You'd better open ...

DOLORES *hesitates.*

I said, open that door.

JUAN *and his two* SISTERS *are let in.*

SECOND SISTER. Here she is!

YERMA. Yes, here I am.

JUAN. What are you doing here? I should wake the whole
village. Then they could see what my wife's doing to my
good name. That's what I should do. But I'll have to
keep my mouth shut even though it chokes me.

YERMA. Wake the village. I'll be glad. Wake the dead for
all I care, and let them see for themselves that I'm guilty
of nothing, nothing.

JUAN. I'm not putting up with any more. You trick me,
you cheat me and because I'm a straightforward hard-
working man you think you can get away with it.

DOLORES. Juan!

JUAN. Shut your mouth.

DOLORES. She's done nothing wrong!

JUAN. She's been doing me wrong ever since the day we
married. Fixing me with her black looks, and keeping

me awake all night sighing on the pillow.

YERMA. Hold your tongue!

JUAN. I can't take any more. You need nerves of steel to
live with a woman who hates your guts and who spends
her nights roaming the streets. And looking for what,
I'd like to know? Looking for what? There's men
enough on every street corner. Don't try to tell me she
goes out to pick flowers.

YERMA. I won't hear it! I won't listen to another word!
You – and all your family – go on as if you were the only
people in the world with any pride. My family are proud
too, let me tell you. There are no skeletons in our
family cupboard . . . Come here and smell my clothes.
Come on! See for yourself if there is anything that isn't
yours – that doesn't smell of you. You can strip me
naked in the square and spit in my face in front of
everybody. You can do anything you like with me
because I'm your wife, but don't you dare suggest that
any other man has been where only you have been.

JUAN. It's not me. It's you and your carrying on. The
whole village is beginning to talk. And they're talking
loud and clear. Whenever I go anywhere people go
quiet. When I go to the mill to weigh flour people stop
talking. And even when I lie awake at night in the fields,
the trees stop rustling their branches.

YERMA. An ill wind can flatten the corn, but does that
mean the seed is bad?

JUAN. And what sort of ill wind is it drives a woman from
her house at all hours of the day and night.

YERMA (*seizing hold of* JUAN). I'm looking for you! I'm
looking for you! I'm looking for you, day and night and
nowhere can I find you. It's your heart that I want.

JUAN. Get your hands off me!

YERMA. Don't throw me off. Hold me! Love me!

JUAN. Get off.

YERMA. Look at me! Left as lonely as the moon, searching in the sky for herself. Look at me!

He looks at her, then tears himself roughly away.

JUAN. Once and for all, leave me alone!

YERMA *falls to the ground.*

DOLORES. Juan!

YERMA (*in a loud lament*). Where I looked for carnations I found only a wall – a cold stone wall to beat my head against. Ay! Ay!

JUAN. Be quiet and let's go.

DOLORES. God save us!

YERMA (*shouting*). Damn my father for leaving me a hundred sons in his blood! And damn my mother for leaving me searching among blind alleys and blank walls!

JUAN. Be quiet!

DOLORES. Keep your voices down! There's people coming.

YERMA. What do I care! At least leave me a voice in this well of despair . . . (*She rises*). And, leave me my body too, just in case a little one might some day come from it to sweeten this morning air.

Voices are heard.

DOLORES. They're coming this way.

JUAN. Silence!

YERMA. Yes, that's it! Silence. Silence above all.

JUAN. Come on. Let's go, quickly.

YERMA. That's it then! That's it! What's the use screaming to Heaven. It's one thing to love with your mind but if your body won't do it – then let it rot. That's it. I'm not going to fight any more. From now on it's silence.

She goes out.

Curtain.

Scene Two

Outside a shrine high in the mountains. In the foreground rugs are spread over wheels of a cart forming a rustic tent where YERMA *is. Barefoot* WOMEN *enter in procession on their way to the shrine to deposit their offerings. On stage is the* PAGAN WOMAN.

Song before curtain rises.

> When you were a virgin
> I was not allowed to see you
> But now that you are married
> I will strip you naked
> In the dark of midnight
> My little married pilgrim.

PAGAN WOMAN (*sarcastically*). Been having a good swig of Holy Water?

FIRST OLD WOMAN. Why not?

PAGAN WOMAN. We'll soon see what the old saint can do then, won't we?

FIRST OLD WOMAN. We believe in him even if you don't.

PAGAN WOMAN. Every year women come to pray for children. And every year more and more men come to this pilgrimage – on their own. Now I wonder why that could be, eh? (*She laughs.*)

FIRST OLD WOMAN. Well, why do you come here?

PAGAN WOMAN. Why do I come? I like to watch what's going on. And keep an eye on that son of mine. You remember last year, those two lads killing each other over some married woman. Anyway, I like a bit of an outing.

FIRST OLD WOMAN. May God forgive you! (*Exits.*)

PAGAN WOMAN. Him!

She leaves. MARIA *enters with* FIRST GIRL.

FIRST GIRL. Did she get here in the end?

MARIA. There's their cart. I can tell you I had a terrible job trying to persuade them. She's spent the whole month just sitting in a chair. I'm scared. She's got some idea in her head, I don't know what, but I can't help feeling it's bad.

FIRST GIRL. I came with my sister. She's been coming for eight years and still nothing.

MARIA. Those that are meant to have children have them.

FIRST GIRL. That's what I always say.

Voices are heard.

MARIA. I've never cared for this Romería. Let's go down to the threshing floor where there's more people about.

FIRST GIRL. Last year some boys started messing about with my sister when it got dark – pinching her breasts and that.

MARIA. You always hear stories like that.

FIRST GIRL. There's more than forty casks of wine behind the shrine.

MARIA. They're pouring in from the mountains – the men, and every one of them single.

> MARIA *and the* GIRL *leave.* YERMA *appears with six* WOMEN *in procession, all barefoot, carrying candles. Night falls.*

YERMA. Lord may the rose come to flower,
don't leave it to wither in darkness.

SECOND WOMAN. May the yellow rose
blossom in her barren flesh.

YERMA. In the wombs of your suppliants
let the fire of the earth burn bright.

WOMEN'S CHORUS. Lord, may the rose come to flower
don't leave it to wither in darkness.

They all kneel.

YERMA. In the garden of Heaven
  Grow roses and roses,
  Halcyon roses,
  The rose tree of life.
  With the first rays of dawn,
  Comes an archangel to guard her
  With stormy wings
  And melancholy eyes.
  Round its leaves fountains
  Of warm milk play and
  Wet the faces of the silent stars.
  Lord, open your rose tree
  Within my barren flesh.

  They stand up.

SECOND WOMAN. Lord, cool with your hand
  the burning coals of her cheeks.
YERMA. Listen to the prayer of this penitent
  on your holy pilgrimage.
  Open your rose within my body
  though it be covered with a thousand thorns.
CHORUS. Lord, may the rose come to flower.
  don't leave it to wither in darkness.
YERMA. Within my barren flesh
  let flower the wondrous rose.

  They leave. Noise breaks out and GIRLS *enter running from
  left trailing long ribbons. From the right come three more
  looking over their shoulders. There is a crescendo of voices and a
  noise of all sorts of bells – harness, cattle, pandaretta etc.*

  The noise reaches a crescendo as the two MASKED DANCERS
  *appear – male and female. The masks they wear are not
  grotesque but of great simplicity and elemental beauty. The*
  MALE *brandishes a bull's horn and the* FEMALE *jangles a
  halter covered in bells.*

Back stage fills with people barracking and applauding. It is now quite dark.

CHILDREN. The Devil and his Wife! The Devil and his Wife!

This sequence is a mixture of 'coplas' sung or declaimed, interspersed with coarse comments from the crowd. The 'coplas' are accompanied by guitars and/or the rhythmical clapping of hands.

FEMALE MASKER. In the mountain river
  The sad wife went to bathe.
  Up her naked body
  Climbed little water-snails.
  The early breeze of morning
  By the sandy river bank
  Set her cheeks on fire
  And shivers down her spine.
  Ah, how naked she was,
  That young woman in the river!
BOY. And how she yelled!
FIRST MAN. Nothing like a cool breeze and cold water if you're feeling hot!
SECOND MAN. If it's worth having, it's worth waiting for!
FIRST MAN. Everything comes to him that waits!
SECOND MAN. Even with a dry crack and a pasty face!
FEMALE MASKER. When falls the starry night
  And the rest of the world is in bed.
  This night of our Romeria
  'Twill be petticoats over the head!
BOY. How quickly the night has fallen
  Will you look how quick it's come!
  Look up there into the darkness
  How black the water falls!

  Guitars begin to strike up.

MALE MASKER (*getting up and making obscene gestures with the*

bull's horn). Ah, how white is the sad nude wife!
O, how she moans among the oleanders!
No thought now for carnations and poppies
When a man spreads his cape on the ground.

If you come to the Romería
To pray for a filled-out belly
Don't come to it dressed for a funeral
But put on your best Sunday blouse.
Come alone by the path near the wall
To where the fig-trees grow thickest
And I'll furrow you into the ground
Till the cocks shout break of day.
Ah how she shines!
Ah, how she shone!
Ah, how that woman came swinging her hips!

FEMALE MASKER.
Ah, how love garlands the secret places
And pierces them with thrusts of molten gold.

MALE MASKER. Seven times she groaned,
Nine times she rose,
And fifteen times they coupled
Under the jasmine in the orange grove.

THIRD MAN. Now give it the horn!

SECOND MAN. No rose without a thorn!

FIRST MAN. Ah, how that woman swings her hips!

MALE MASKER. At our Romería
The men have their say.
They're rams to a man
And they have their own way,
And the women they fancy
They'll soon enough lay.

BOY. Whirl it about a bit!

SECOND MAN. Shove it up a bit!

MALE MASKER. Take a look at that fine girl naked in
the river!

FIRST MAN. She bends like a reed.

MALE MASKER. And wilts like a flower.

MEN. Who takes first pick of the girls?

MALE MASKER. Whoever warms up the dancing
And thrusts life in the body of a ripe married woman.

They go out singing gaily to the clapping of hands.

In the garden of Heaven,
Grow roses and roses,
Halcyon roses,
The rose tree of life.

Two GIRLS *run past screaming. The* PAGAN WOMAN *comes in full of jollity.*

PAGAN WOMAN (*shouting after the revellers*). I hope you'll give us a chance to get some sleep now. It may be your turn next. (*She sees* YERMA *enter.*) You!

YERMA *is downcast and silent.*

What brought you here then?

YERMA. I don't know myself.

PAGAN WOMAN. Still not convinced, eh? What about your husband?

YERMA *seems exhausted and preoccupied with some fixed idea.*

YERMA. He's over there.

PAGAN WOMAN. What's he up to?

YERMA. Drinking.

YERMA *raises her hands to her forehead.*

Ay!

PAGAN WOMAN. Less of all that. Show some spirit. Listen, I can tell you something now that I couldn't before.

YERMA. What can you tell me I don't know already?

PAGAN WOMAN. Something that's no secret to anyone. It's as plain as daylight. Your husband's to blame.

D'you hear me? Cut off my hand if I tell a lie. Not his father, nor his grandfather, not even his great-grandfather were proved real men. A miracle that any one of them put a girl in the family way. They've nothing but gobs of spit between the lot of them. But you're different. The countryside for miles around is thick with your kin. Oh, it's a black curse on a lovely girl like you!

YERMA. A black curse! A blight on ripe corn!

PAGAN WOMAN. Well, then . . . You've got feet, haven't you? What's stopping you?

YERMA. Stopping me?

PAGAN WOMAN. Yes. When I saw you here it came to me in a flash. Women come here to find a man, don't they? And the old Saint works the miracle. Now, my house needs a young woman in it and my son is a full-blooded lad. He's like me in that. He's just up there behind the shrine waiting. If you get on with him the three of us can all live together. The bed-springs will turn into babies in no time – you'll see. Why the house still smells of babies. Don't mind what people say. And as for your husband, we can take care of him.

YERMA. Stop it! Stop it! I could never think of it – never! D'you think I could just go and live with another man? What about my pride, my self-respect? I couldn't do a thing like that any more than water can flow uphill or the full moon shine at midday . . . No, I have to go my own way. Can you see me become another man's whore, obey his every little whim? I know myself, and I know I never could. So don't speak about it ever again.

PAGAN WOMAN. When you're thirsty, you're glad of water.

YERMA. What good in a desert is a drop of water? It's not my body that thirsts, it's my heart.

PAGAN WOMAN (*shouting*). Then go to hell in your own

way! A barren woman's no better than a bunch of dried thistles.

YERMA (*shouting*). Barren . . . barren, I know I am! But you don't have to torture me. Don't torture me with it like children with a helpless animal. Ever since my marriage the word 'barren' has been in my thoughts but this is the first time I have heard it, the first time it has been thrown in my face. Now I know it's true.

PAGAN WOMAN. As if I care. And you needn't think I'll have any trouble getting a woman for my son.

The PAGAN WOMAN *goes. A great chorus of song is heard in the distance. As* YERMA *goes towards the cart,* JUAN *suddenly appears from behind it.*

YERMA. Have you been here all the time?

JUAN. Yes.

YERMA. Eavesdropping?

JUAN. You can call it that.

YERMA. You heard everything?

JUAN. Yes.

YERMA. And much good may it do you. Go off and join the fun, why don't you? (*She sits down on the rugs.*)

JUAN. Because I've got to speak.

YERMA. Speak then.

JUAN. Once and for all stop crying for the moon, for things that are only in the air and in the darkness of your mind – things that have nothing to do with real life.

YERMA (*with dramatic surprise*). With real life? That have nothing to do with real life!

JUAN. Yes. We can't control things that haven't happened.

YERMA (*violently*). Go on! Go on!

JUAN. This thing means nothing to me, d'you understand! Absolutely nothing! There! It's time I said it. What matters to me is what I can hold in the palm of my hand and see with my own two eyes.

YERMA (*rising to her knees in desperation*). There! There! So now at last you've said it. When the truth remains unspoken you can still believe it doesn't really exist, but once it is out how loud and terrible it sounds.

JUAN (*coming closer*). Listen to me! (*He tries to make her get up.*) Face facts. There are enough women who'd be happy in your shoes. Life is simpler without kids, and I like it that way. And it's nobody's fault.

YERMA. Then what d'you want me for?

JUAN. For yourself.

YERMA. Oh, yes. Of course! A home, a bit of comfort and a woman now and again. That's all you ever wanted. Aren't I right?

JUAN. Isn't that what everybody wants?

YERMA. And nothing more? What about your son?

JUAN. I've just told you. You heard me. I've said that means nothing to me.

YERMA. And do you never think how much it means to me?

JUAN. Never.

They are both now on the ground.

YERMA. Is there no hope then?

JUAN. No. None.

YERMA. You won't ever change?

JUAN. Never. Accept it.

YERMA. Childless.

JUAN. Peaceful. You and me together in peace and happiness. Hold me! (*He holds her.*)

YERMA. What do you want?

JUAN. I want you. In the moonlight you look so beautiful.

YERMA. That look in your eyes – hungry for flesh but not for me.

JUAN. Kiss me . . . like this . . . and this.

YERMA. That, never . . . never like that.

YERMA *gives a shriek and seizes* JUAN *by the throat. She forces him backwards and slowly she strangles the life out of him. Again the singing is heard from the Romeria.*

YERMA. Barren, yes. Barren and alone forever, now it's certain. Maybe now I shall rest. Maybe now I shall sleep, not start up in the night wondering if some new life's quickening in me. Alone, alone with this barren body forever. (*She gets up. People start to gather round.*) Don't come near me! What do you want to know, that I've killed him? Yes, I've killed him. I've killed my son.

More people crowd forward. Once more singing is heard from the Romeria.

Curtain.

Note on the translation
Yerma revisited

On the face of it my credentials for presuming to translate Lorca's *Yerma* are pretty slim. I am not an academic hispanist nor, alas, am I a poet. True I am a working playwright but that in itself would not be enough. The only qualification that gives me – perhaps uniquely among English playwrights – a right to think I could do it is that I was for ten years an Andalusian farmer living not many miles away from the Garcia Lorca home at Fuente Vaqueros. For most of those years I spoke to few people (outside my family) other than the local farmers and villagers. But from them I learnt many things, not only of an agricultural nature. Above all I learnt something of the social and anthropological background to Lorca's work.*

I brought my family to Spain in September 1967 to make a film for the BBC: a dramatization of Lorca's Andalusian poetry. I spoke no Spanish but with me was a friend, the actor Carlos Douglas, who despite his name, was – and is – a full-blooded Andaluz from La Linea. He played the double role of leading actor and interpreter. In between takes of our film we decided to translate *Yerma*: Carlos doing a literal transation which I then put into plain English. We never even attempted the songs and poems which at the time seemed beyond us.

Seven years later, by which time I spoke not Castellano but fluent Andaluz, I came across our old script. Familiar now with the idiom and, more particularly with the mores

---

* *The Mad Pomegranate & The Praying Mantis*, by Peter Luke, Mantis Press & Colin Smythe Ltd., 1984

of the country people, I decided to go back to the beginning. What I wanted to do was to read into Lorca's lines much that I now knew from experience. By this time too, I felt bold enough to attempt the songs and poems. More than anything I wanted to produce an *actable* version which an English company might wish to perform. So I went to work. When I did, I realised that I was not only dealing with 'country matters', but with a subject that is today of greater concern to more women than ever before, the control of their own fecundity.

Peter Luke, 1987